INSTRUCTOR'S RESOURCE GUIDE
TO ACCOMPANY

IDEAS AND STYLES IN THE WESTERN MUSICAL TRADITION

INSTRUCTOR'S RESOURCE GUIDE TO ACCOMPANY

IDEAS AND STYLES IN THE WESTERN MUSICAL TRADITION

Douglass Seaton
Florida State University

Mayfield Publishing Company
Mountain View, California
London • Toronto

International Standard Book Number: 0-87484-957-8

Manufactured in the United States of America

10 9 8 7 6 5 4 3 2 1

Mayfield Publishing Company
1240 Villa Street
Mountain View, California 94041

CONTENTS

INTRODUCTION

TEACHING STRATEGIES

ORIENTATION OF THE TEXTBOOK

Ideas and Styles in the Western Musical Tradition gives a concise history of the Western "classical" tradition in music. It deals with both music in relation to general cultural history and the history of musical styles. Its fundamental assumption is that one studies the history of music to become a better performer, composer, or listener by understanding the nature of musical thinking. It does not attempt to serve as a comprehensive reference of music-history information but rather presents a discursive survey of musical thought.

The text therefore concentrates on (1) the most significant historical, philosophical, and artistic influences on music in the various periods of music history and (2) the major principles of and models for musical expression—ethos and paideia in classical antiquity; worship and the mathematical symbolization of cosmic order in the Middle Ages; poetic mimesis in the Renaissance; affective rhetoric in the Baroque; structural and emotional drama in the Classic and Romantic periods; and the multiplicity of alternative models since the turn of the last century. The approach includes all the major composers, introducing them in connection with their original contributions to musical thinking or as examples of important directions in musical culture or style; it does not, however, attempt to incorporate every composer merely as a (futile) attempt at thoroughness. Likewise, the book deals with specific significant works when their place in the history of musical ideas warrants it, but it does not interrupt the flow of its discussion for lists of composers' works, nor does it make detailed analyses of individual pieces.

In placing its emphasis on musical thought rather than on historical data, the book takes two important approaches. One is to emphasize the position of music in the humanities, through consideration of philosophical and artistic movements. Numerous citations and quotations from writers and artists (as well as from musicians) in all periods support the ideas discussed, not as gratuitous "enhancement" but as part of the body of the text. In addition, as a consequence of the consistent pursuit of the models that the various musical movements have adopted for musical expression, the treatment of musical styles, forms, and significant works is oriented toward exploring how the fundamental expressive models were employed, varied, and developed.

Illustrations show relevant works of art and architecture, unfamiliar instruments, and significant musical sources such as manuscripts. They specifically support points made in the text and have substantial captions.

Ideas and Styles was designed for a one-year course in music history for music majors in the middle years of college. It presupposes some knowledge of basic music theory (for example, intervals, simple figured bass, the elementary tonal chord functions, and the smaller standard forms), but it is not highly technical. Graduate music students who need a review of music history have used it, and it might also interest nonspecialists with as little background as a standard introductory music course.

ONE-YEAR SYLLABUS

The syllabus outlined here is designed for an academic year of thirty weeks with three class sessions per week (plus two major examination periods). Instructors will naturally need to adapt it to their own situations.

Week	Session	Material to be covered
1	1	Chapter 1: Music in Greek life and thought
	2	Greek music theory
	3	Roman contributions
2	1	Chapter 2: Jewish and early Christian music
	2	Regional traditions
	3	Chapter 3: Liturgy
3	1	Chant aesthetics and style
	2	Chant theory
	3	Later developments from chant
4	1	Chapter 4: Medieval secular song
	2	Instruments
	3	Chapter 5: Organum to 1150
5	1	Notre Dame style
	2	Motet and notation
	3	Chapter 6: Mensuration and isorhythm
6	1	French music
	2	Italian and English music
	3	UNIT TEST

CUMULATIVE EXAMINATION

ALTERNATIVE SYLLABUS

The thirty-week syllabus presented above probably represents the most common situation in American colleges at present. This schedule certainly confronts the teacher who has to cover such a large amount of material in such a short time with a considerable challenge. A more leisurely pace in which the course content can be extended to three semesters, or more frequent meetings, would allow for more discussion, more detailed study of a greater number of scores and recordings, more live music played in the classroom by students or guest performers, and the addition of supplementary readings. For such a three-semester syllabus the text may most appropriately be divided after Chapter 11 and after Chapter 18.

An accelerated syllabus is also possible. This would require students to do more work on their own, especially studying music (since that eats up large quantities of class time). The following indicates how the material might be compressed into a single fifteen-week semester:

Week	Session	Material to be covered
1	1	Chapter 1: Music in Greek life and thought
	2	Greek music theory, Roman ideas
	3	Chapter 2: Early Christian music
2	1	Chapter 3: Liturgy, Chant
	2	Chant theory, Later developments
	3	Chapter 4: Medieval secular music
3	1	Chapter 5: Polyphony to ca. 1200
	2	Thirteenth-century polyphony
	3	Chapter 6: Ars nova
4	1	Later fourteenth-century music
	2	Chapter 7: Early Renaissance
	3	Chapter 8: Franco-Netherlands style
5	1	Regional genres and styles
	2	Chapter 9: Instrumental music
	3	Chapter 10: Reformation
6	1	Counter-Reformation
	2	Chapter 11: Italian music
	3	English and French music
7	1	Chapter 12: Baroque aesthetics and style
	2	Chapter 13: Secular vocal genres
	3	Sacred music, Instrumental music

8	1	Chapter 14: Regional genres and styles
	2	Instrumental music and forms
	3	Chapter 15: French and Italian opera
9	1	Handel and Bach
	2	MIDTERM TEST
	3	Chapter 16: The Galant and Empfindsamkeit
10	1	Chapter 17: Classicism, Opera
	2	The sonata idea
	3	Chapter 18: Instrumental genres
11	1	Opera, Beethoven
	2	Chapter 19: Romanticism, Beethoven after 1802
	3	Early Romantic song, opera
12	1	Chapter 20: Mature Romantic opera
	2	Song, Piano music
	3	Orchestral music
13	1	Chapter 21: Music of the Future, Wagner
	2	Late Romanticism, Post-Romanticism
	3	Exoticism, Nationalism
14	1	Chapter 22: Impressionism, Primitivism
	2	Expressionism, Ives
	3	Chapter 23: Twelve-tone method, Serialism
15	1	Tonal styles after World War I
	2	Chapter 24: Total control, Electronic music
	3	Avant-garde, Popular music

FINAL EXAMINATION

LISTENING AND SCORE STUDY

The core of the music history course must be music. As a general rule of thumb, the teacher might aim for a syllabus in which each class session and each daily assignment would include at least some study of scores and some listening.

Students need to know what is expected of them as they listen and read scores. A clear, systematic approach that requires them actively to engage the identity and place of a piece in history and to consider the work from the viewpoint of all the common elements of style will help them to think about the music thoroughly and creatively. A simple "Score/Listening Worksheet" is provided as part of the supplementary material for *Ideas and Styles* in order to suggest how this can be achieved. Some early class time should be devoted to demonstrating this or some other system for music study; later on students can prepare the music on their own in anticipation of or as follow-up after a class session. Worksheets can also be used as homework assignments or quizzes to check students' analysis skills.

Naturally the teacher must know what analytical skills can be expected of the students. He or she will probably have to provide some analytical guidance as well. The historical development of music partly teaches its own analysis, however, in the sense that the developments of style raise new analytical problems in step-by-step fashion. In a historical study students first encounter notes on the staff, then simple melodic forms, and eventually larger forms determined by harmonic structure. Chronologically the use of harmonic intervals and the concept of consonance and dissonance in two-part music precede intervallic harmony in more parts, then figured bass, and, still later, chord functions.

The standard approach to the teaching of music theory has long been to begin with functional harmony and four-voice partwriting. As a result students may be inclined to apply anachronistic modes of thinking and inappropriate methods of analysis to pre-eighteenth-century music. They may find the need for alternative analytical techniques intimidating. The teacher should emphasize that different styles require different approaches. He or she should assure students that although earlier music might seem foreign, the basic analytical techniques it calls for (aside from some late medieval arcana!) are within the students' reach.

Analysis is not an end in itself. The purpose of analysis is to stimulate and support critical thinking. When the student has thoroughly studied the musical content and structure of a piece, he or she must then go on to consider such questions as what ideas it embodies and how it relates to its historical context, and to evaluate it critically.

LIVE MUSIC

Exposure to live music will make an important contribution to students' understanding of musical thinking. Within the classroom setting students should perform as much as possible, beginning with chant and including all sorts of vocal and instrumental chamber music. They will grasp such concepts as antiphonal and responsorial scoring and will gain a sense of the interaction between performers in chamber music, even in somewhat unpolished live performances, that cannot come from recordings.

Students should also be expected to attend performances outside their course work; written concert reports or performance reviews may be used to encourage attendance and to keep the students' attention focused. In particular they should be exposed to musical performances that have an essentially visual component, including opera, dance, and worship services. When, as in many communities, live opera and ballet are only rare treats, film or videotape recordings of opera and ballet can provide a compromise.

ORAL PARTICIPATION

Every college professor has known and would like to be able to emulate those marvelous public lecturers whose courses are a series of stimulating, profound, perfectly organized, elegantly literary, and charmingly witty monologues. But one of the most important functions of the music history survey course in the curriculum is to encourage students to express their own ideas and responses to music. Part of the music history teacher's task is helping students to cultivate the verbal, analytical, and critical skills required for intelligent and effective discourse about the subject. In very large classes this is extremely difficult, so—if at all possible—class sizes should be kept small enough to allow student participation. Active participation by students can probably be achieved in classes of up to around forty, if the instructor makes this a priority.

Oral reports to the class by students provide opportunities for developing their confidence and comfort as well as their skills in discussing music. These can be as formal or informal as the teacher desires and as the students seem to need. The teacher may wish to plan and assign series of oral reports on a regular schedule through the term. On the other hand, when a student raises a question in class, the teacher may wish to respond, "That is an excellent question, and I'm not sure of the answer myself. Would you do some research on that and give us a very short report next time? I'll meet you after class and give you some ideas how to get started."

In any event, for several reasons it is important that oral reports be kept short. Students should not find these assignments burdensome as well as scary. Students will sometimes rebel against the idea that they could be tested on material the bulk of which is presented, perhaps unevenly, by their peers. Any class session should not be dominated by a single student. And the need to be concise will make students critique their material and keep their thoughts in order.

In addition to assigned reports, the instructor should allow plenty of time for student responses to the music and ideas presented in the course. A few simple formulas for questions to students will help: "What do you think about this passage?" "Does this idea make good sense to you?" "What seems to be most important in this composer's way of thinking?" Particularly effective are "how" and "why" questions: "How is the texture kept clear in this piece?" "How does the music relate to the words?" "Why did this composer not compose in this particular genre?" "Why does this piece not conform to the standard patterns of musical structure in its time?"

In responding to students' answers, the teacher should reinforce the value of their participation and their ideas. A good answer should be praised. A wayward answer should not be rejected in such a way that the student is discouraged from speaking up again. Rather the teacher might ask a follow-up question: "That's an interesting theory, but how would you reconcile that with our earlier observation that . . .?" Alternatively one can stimulate conversation among students by passing the question on to the next student: "So-and-so, do you agree?" "Can you suggest another explanation?" "Could you expand on that?"

Eventually one wants the students to raise the questions themselves. If they do not do so, the teacher should ask them directly to pose questions. He or she might simply ask "What kinds of issues does this music raise?" or "What would you have liked to ask the composer?" Students can also be assigned to bring prepared questions to each class, based on their reading, listening, and score study.

A music history course that encourages lively student participation will not be as tidy, as even and thorough in its coverage of the material, or as easy for the instructor as one that consists of neatly packaged lectures. It will, however, produce students who understand better how to think critically about music and who can express their ideas well.

WRITTEN ASSIGNMENTS

Just as music history serves to provide music students the opportunity to develop their oral communication skills, it generally also functions as the main area in the curriculum for them to work on research and written expression in their field. A well-organized and varied program of writing is essential to the syllabus. The Appendix to *Ideas and Styles* gives some guidelines for students on writing about music.

Students should begin with short, simple essays that allow them to write straightforward, direct sentences and paragraphs. Such an essay could be, for instance, a descriptive report on a single short piece or a report on a composer's life. In reading such an essay, the teacher should evaluate primarily the clarity, accuracy, and organization of the students' statements.

A second stage in developing the students' writing about music could be a critical comparison of two pieces, such as two settings of the same text. The essay should produce a convincing argument supported by analytical observations, logical reasoning, and good musical judgment.

Teachers may wish to draw on the Questions for Reflection that appear at the end of each chapter of *Ideas and Styles* as topics for student essays. In these cases students should attempt to incorporate references to specific music in order to show the applications of the issues and ideas raised in their essays.

The culmination of the writing component of the music history course should be a formal research paper. Familiarizing students with scholarly methods and the materials of library research is one of the most important contributions the course will make to their futures; it should not be slighted. The instructor may wish to lead students through the research process in stages, from the formulation of a topic through the collection of bibliography, procedures for note-taking, outlining, and draft-writing, to the preparation of the final typescript.

SUGGESTED GRADING PROCEDURE

Each teacher and the situation in each institution determine priorities for evaluating students' accomplishment. The following plan can, of course, be adjusted for each case, though each of its components should be included:

Daily participation, including homework assignments	25%
Essays, research paper	25%
Unit tests	25%
Cumulative examination	25%

THE INSTRUCTOR'S MANUAL

The following chapters of this Instructor's Manual offer summaries of the important contents of each chapter of *Ideas and Styles* and suggest various teaching activities. Each chapter is organized as follows:

1. Chapter overview. Here the main points of the chapter are summarized in a few paragraphs.

2. Objectives. This section identifies the most important ideas for the student to understand. It includes issues concerning both the relation of music to history and the development of musical thinking.

3. Terms, names, and concepts. These lists show each chapter's new technical vocabulary, names of leading composers and musical thinkers, and some terms for principal ideas.

4. Classroom approaches, assignments, and topics for discussion. A considerable variety of assignments and class activities are suggested, from which the teacher can choose and adapt those best suited to his or her needs. Each assignment or activity should lead to discussion of the music and ideas involved.

5. Music for study. Each chapter includes a selection of examples from several anthologies for historical study. For each work some important features of style are identified and anthologies that include the work are listed. In appropriate cases, recordings have been included as well.
   The items included here have been chosen for teachability and/or availability. In most cases alternative examples will serve

to make the same points. The teacher who wishes to use a single anthology of music will find that the style features given here can be illustrated from the items in any well-conceived collection. The remarks that are specific to pieces selected here will suggest what to look for in analyzing comparable examples.

6.   Sample test questions. Three types of questions are offered. The present author prefers fill-in to multiple choice format, because in practice we do not live in a world where we select from lists of answers and because it is pedagogically dubious to show students several incorrect responses for each correct one. For instructors in situations where classes are large, where tests must be taken in the shortest possible time, or where grading must be automated, multiple-choice answers are provided here. An answer key is given at the end of the chapter.

In the case of true-false questions, a statement of justification or amplification should be required. This discourages mere guessing and gives the teacher a clearer sense of whether students genuinely understand the material. Sample statements are included in the answer key provided, though there are not single correct answers in these cases.

Tests should also evaluate the student's ability to think and communicate about music. A few topics for short essays are suggested for each chapter. The Questions for Reflection at the end of each chapter of the text may also be adapted as test questions, as may some of the suggestions for Classroom Approaches in this workbook.

All tests should include some listening and score reading. A simple formula works well for questions on recorded or score examples: The student should be expected to identify the genre of the music heard or seen, its historical position, the name of the composer (and for standard masterpieces, the title of the work), and one or more stylistic traits or musical principles it illustrates. For more advanced students a paragraph or brief essay on a musical example may be appropriate.

ABBREVIATIONS FOR ANTHOLOGIES CITED

Scores

(An asterisk indicates that there is a companion collection of recordings with the same title.)

AAM	*Analytical Anthology of Music*, ed. Ralph Turek (New York: Knopf, 1984)
AM	*Anthology of Music* (Cologne: Arno Volk Verlag)
AMM	*Anthology of Medieval Music*, ed. Richard Hoppin (New York: Norton, 1978)

AMSS	*Anthology of Musical Structure and Style*, ed. Mary H. Wennerstrom (Englewood Cliffs, N.J.: Prentice-Hall, 1983)
ARM	*Anthology of Romantic Music*, ed. Leon Plantinga (New York: Norton, 1984)
ATCM	*Anthology of Twentieth-Century Music*, 2d ed., ed. Mary H. Wennerstrom (Englewood Cliffs, N.J.: Prentice-Hall, 1988)
* EMH	*The European Musical Heritage: 800-1750*, ed. Sarah Fuller (New York: Knopf, 1987)
HAM	*Historical Anthology of Music*, 2 vols., ed. Archibald T. Davison and Willi Apel (Cambridge, Mass.: Harvard University Press, 1949)
HAMW	*Historical Anthology of Music by Women*, ed. James R. Briscoe (Bloomington: Indiana University Press, 1987)
MCP	*Music in the Classic Period*, ed. F. E. Kirby (New York: Schirmer, 1979)
* MM	*Masterpieces of Music before 1750*, ed. Carl Parrish and John F. Ohl (New York: Norton, 1951)
MRP	*Music in the Romantic Period*, ed. F. E. Kirby (New York: Schirmer, 1986)
MTC	*Music of the Twentieth Century: An Anthology*, ed. Bryan R. Simms (New York: Schirmer Books, 1986)
* NAWM	*Norton Anthology of Western Music*, 2d ed., ed. Claude V. Palisca (New York: Norton, 1988)
N S	*The Norton Scores: An Anthology for Listeninq*, 2 vols., ed Roger Kamien (New York: Norton, 1984)
OMM	*Medieval Music*, ed. W. Thomas Marrocco and Nicholas Sandon (London: Oxford University Press, 1977)
SSHS	*Study Scores of Historical Styles*, 2 vols., ed. Harry B. Lincoln and Stephen Bonta (Englewood Cliffs, N.J.: Prentice-Hall, 1986)
SSMS	*Study Scores of Musical Styles*, ed. Edward R. Lerner (New York: McGraw-Hill, 1968)

Recordings

HEM   *History of European Music*, Denis Stevens, dir. Musical
               Heritage Society, Orpheus OR 349-354 (accompanies
               HAM)

HMS   *History of Music in Sound*, RCA Victor

CHAPTER 1

MUSIC IN CLASSICAL ANTIQUITY

CHAPTER OVERVIEW

The culture of ancient Greece built the foundations for much of Western musical thinking as for Western culture in general. Although little of the music of this culture survives, written documents provide considerable insight into Greek musical life, aesthetics, and theory. The central aesthetic idea of musical ethos made music an important component of the works of both Plato and Aristotle. It also led to the identification of musical styles according to specific style elements.

Greek musicians also developed the important concept of the organization of a vocabulary of discrete pitches according to acoustical principles. The theoretical system arranged the pitches into tetrachords of different genres, making up the Greater Perfect System. Greek scales (tonoi or harmoniai) derived their structure and character by employing the pitch patterns available in different octave segments of the system.

The ancient Romans borrowed much of their musical culture from the Greeks, adapting instruments and practices to their own needs and tastes. In the late Roman period Martianus Capella and Boethius formulated the position of music among the intellectual disciplines and designed models for the study of music that influenced the treatment of music in the educational system throughout the Middle Ages.

OBJECTIVES

1. To give the student an understanding of the meaning of the concept of musical ethos and its application to Greek musical life and musical style.

2. To help the student to understand the nature of and principles underlying the Greek tonal system.

3. To give the student an understanding of how the Romans adapted the styles of Greek music, as a model exemplifying how and why musical change takes place.

4. To introduce the student to the position of music as an intellectual discipline at the beginning of the Middle Ages.

1

TERMS, NAMES, AND CONCEPTS

Pythagoras
Plato
Aristotle
mimesis
ethos
Apollonian, Dionysian
catharsis
kithara, aulos
harmonia
heterophony
tonos
Greater Perfect System
tetrachord
genus
    diatonic
    chromatic
    enharmonic
Martianus Capella
trivium, quadrivium
Anicius Manlius Severinus Boethius
De institutione musica
musica speculativa, musica practica
musicus, cantor
musica mundana, musica humana, musica instrumentalis

CLASSROOM APPROACHES, ASSIGNMENTS, TOPICS FOR DISCUSSION

Ethos

Have students define the principle of ethos in music. Be sure that it is clear to them that the doctrine claims that the effect of the music is to change human character and behavior.

Play a recorded example of ancient Greek music without allowing students to know the text. Have each student write down his or her idea of the musical ethos, then collect the responses and read several of them to the class. Read or distribute copies of the text, and play the music again. Discuss what factors determine the music's ethos and the importance of musical acculturation in understanding music.

Have students discuss the belief in or application of the concept of musical ethos in modern American culture. Ask them to reflect contemporary attitudes toward the ethical effects of rock music. Consider the application of musical ethos in music therapy.

The Greek Musical System

Demonstrate the Greater Perfect System, using the piano keyboard or, if possible, a guitar tuned to six of the seven fixed pitches of the system—i.e., A, B, e, a, b, e', [a'] (or G, A, d, g, a, d', [g']). If desired, notate the pitches of the Greater Perfect System using modern note names or staff notation. This is most easily done using the diatonic pitches as follows:

+   tetrachord   tetrachord   tetrachord   tetrachord

X/4 ---- 1=4 ---- 1/4 ---- 1=4 ---- 1

A/B c - d - e=e f - g - a/b c' - d' - e'=e' f' - g' - a'

(The point can be made that spatial metaphors in our musical vocabulary are somewhat arbitrary, and students may be amused if in discussing the system the terms "up" and "down" are used in reverse of our standard practice, always with simultaneous demonstration so that it is clear what is meant.)

Assign students to compose a melody to an ancient Greek poetic text (in English), using Greek pitch patterns and rhythms derived from those of the words. Examples of appropriate texts may be found among the lyrics of Sappho or the choruses in the plays of Sophocles. Have compositions performed in class, using appropriate instrumental doubling.

Music in the Liberal Arts

Have students compare the organization of the disciplines at your own institution to that of Capella and Boethius. Develop with them some innovative designs for organizing the different disciplines of learning.

Discuss with students the relationship between the scholarly and practical approaches to music in their own experience. To what extent are these two approaches emphasized in your institution, and how are they integrated? How does modern American culture value each aspect of music?

MUSIC FOR STUDY

First Delphic Hymn to Apollo

This is one of the earliest and most substantial examples available. The original notation is illustrated in the textbook in Fig. 1.2.

Style features

Scoring—The performance forces for this music are not specified in the notation. This example provides an excellent first opportunity to discuss the scoring of music when the notation itself does not supply precise information. The presence of text indicates that the performance should be vocal. Because the hymn is addressed to

Apollo, accompaniment with a string instrument would be appropriate, though the text mentions the sounds of both aulos and kithara, suggesting that both are played.

Dynamics—Like scoring, dynamics are not notated. It should be stressed here and in all music up to the Baroque period that performance in regard to dynamics must have been guided by such factors as text, social function, performance conditions. (Students must be aware that it is impossible to have music with "no dynamics.")

Rhythm—Durations are determined by the quantitative values of the Greek text syllables.

Melody—The vocal range is rather wide vocal range. The hymn has somewhat long phrases, based on the poetic text.

Harmony—The example employs the Dorian tonos. Students will easily hear that the first section is diatonic and the second is chromatic.

Texture—The notation indicates monophony, but heterophonic practice seems likely.

Form—The hymn is constructed of distinct poetic and musical stanzas.

Extramusical elements—The work has a religious function as a song of praise.

Scores

HAM 1, 9

* HMS 1, booklet pp. 32–34

Recordings

Musique de la Grèce antique. Atrium musicae de Madrid, Gregorio Paniagua, dir. Harmonia mundi HM 1015. This is a very imaginative recording, presenting all the available fragments of ancient Greek music.

Epitaph of Seikilos

This very brief and simple example comes from a source that is clear and complete.

Style features

The piece is the epitaph for the tomb of Seikilos's wife.

Rhythm is guided by the quantitative values of the Greek text syllables. The vocal range is moderate (1 octave). The phrases are relatively short, governed by the poetic text. The epitaph illustrates the diatonic genus and the Phrygian harmonia. The structure is a single stanza in four phrases, with some resemblances between phrases 2 and 3, and 3 and 4.

Scores

HAM 1, 10
* HMS 1, booklet p. 35
* NAWM 1, 2

Recordings

Musique de la Grèce antique. Atrium musicae de Madrid, Gregorio Paniagua, dir. Harmonia mundi HM 1015.

SAMPLE TEST QUESTIONS

Multiple Choice

1. In ancient Greece, the elements of music were considered to include _____, _____ and _____.

   A. dynamics, instrumentation, harmony
   B. words, melody, rhythm
   C. scoring, texture, text
   D. rhythm, meter, form
   E. poetry, religion, ethos

2. The Greek belief that music can affect the listener's character and behavior is embodied in the doctrine of_____.

   A. aulos
   B. enharmic
   C. ethos
   D. harmonia
   E. mimesis

3. The idea that music, like drama, consisted of an imitation of human action was developed in the philosophy of _____.

   A. Aristotle
   B. Boethius
   C. Capella
   D. Plato
   E. Pythagoras

4. The important Greek instrument associated with the worship of the god Apollo was the_____.

   A. harmonia
   B. catharsis
   C. heterophony
   D. lyre
   E. instrumentalis

5. The aulos was a_____instrument.

   A. woodwind
   B. brass
   C. percussion
   D. string
   E. keyboard

6. The three genera of tetrachords in the Greek system of music theory included_____.

   A. chromatic
   B. diatonic
   C. humana
   D. A and B only
   E. A, B, and C

7. The total pitch spectrum of the Greek music theorists was laid out according to the_____.

   A. tetrachord
   B. musica speculativa
   C. tonos
   D. Greater Perfect System
   E. quadrivium

8. The Greek tonos was a kind of_____.

   A. tone
   B. scale
   C. mode
   D. instrument
   E. epic poem

9. The fundamental groupings of the liberal arts in the education system from the late Roman period through the Middle Ages were the work of_____.

   A. Aristotle
   B. Boethius
   C. Capella

D. Dorian
E. none of the above

10. The great Roman scholar Boethius discussed music in his treatise
_____.

A. *Republic*
B. *Poetics*
C. *Politics*
D. *De institutione musica*
E. Greater Perfect System

True-False/Justification

1. Relatively little music notation has survived to allow study of Greek music.

2. Just as much of the sculpture and architecture of ancient Greece has survived, philosophical and theoretical discussions from the time concentrate more on those arts than on music.

3. As philosophers, Plato and Aristotle made a clear distinction between music and poetry.

4. Greek music often served to support other cultural activities.

5. The term *Dionysian* is used to characterize music that seems emotional and sensual.

6. The basis of the Greek system of music theory was the octave.

7. Roman music was generally more restrained than that of the Greeks.

8. The Romans developed brass instruments more than the Greeks had done.

9. Music in the late Roman scheme of human knowledge and study was closely allied with mathematical disciplines.

10. There was no place for singing in Boethius's classification of music into three divisions.

Short Essay

Compare the musical ideas of Plato and Aristotle.

Explain how the major principles discussed by Greek philosophers and theorists would be incorporated into the divisions of musical study as outlined by Boethius.

ANSWERS TO SAMPLE TEST QUESTIONS

Multiple Choice

1. B   words, melody, rhythm
2. C   ethos
3. A   Aristotle
4. D   lyre
5. A   woodwind
6. D   A and B only
7. D   Greater Perfect System
8. B   scale
9. C   Capella
10. D   *De institutione musica*

True-False/Justification

1. T   Only a few dozen, mostly fragmentary, sources are extant.

2. F   Music is discussed much more than the visual arts in Greek philosophy and theory.

3. F   They include words as a component of music and melody and rhythm as parts of poetry.

4. T   Music was important in the drama and in religious ritual.

5. T   The worship of Dionysus was emotional and orgiastic.

6. F   The Greek theoretical system was based on the tetrachord.

7. F   The Romans preferred large ensembles and cultivated virtuosity.

8. T   They used them in connection with their extensive military campaigns.

9. T   Music belonged to the quadrivium, together with arithmetic, geometry, and astronomy.

10. F   The division musica instrumentalis included vocal music.

CHAPTER 2

THE EARLY CHRISTIAN PERIOD

CHAPTER OVERVIEW

After three centuries of persecution of Christians by the Roman empire, the Edict of Milan proclaimed that religious toleration and Christianity could grow freely. The church became the main repository for culture in general and for music in the following centuries.

Christian worship and music practices were inherited from Jewish tradition. Judaism provided the foundations for Christian worship practice, music, and traits of musical style.

As Christianity spread, various regional repertoires and styles arose. The Eastern branch of the church, centered in Byzantium, produced a very elaborate musical culture. Several different areas of western Europe also cultivated their own music and musical practices.

OBJECTIVES

1. To introduce the student to the historical and theological background for music in early Christian church.

2. To acquaint the student with the most important elements of Judaeo-Christian worship practices.

3. To help the student understand the formation of different regional musical styles and repertoires as a model for cultural diversification as a musical-historical process.

TERMS, NAMES, AND CONCEPTS

Edict of Milan
St. Ambrose
St. Augustine
psalm
canticle
hymn
direct, responsorial, antiphonal
mode
Byzantine

kontakion
kanon
echos
Old Roman
Ambrosian
Celtic
Gallican
Mozarabic

CLASSROOM APPROACHES, ASSIGNMENTS, TOPICS FOR DISCUSSION

The Role of Music in Religion

Read with the class the entire (brief) section of St. Augustine's *Confessions* that deals with music and the temptations of hearing. Identify the pros and cons of music in religious experience according to Augustine. Discuss why music is a nearly universal component of religions throughout the world.

Hold a debate in class on one of the following subjects: "RESOLVED: That music for Christian worship should be free to employ any musical style" or "RESOLVED: That church music must be under the guidance and final authority of theologians."

Elements of Worship in the Judaeo-Christian Tradition

Assign students to collect service bulletins, worship folders, or programs from local churches and synagogues. Identify the following elements and practices: prayer, scripture reading, teaching, almsgiving; canticles, psalms, hymns; direct, responsorial, and antiphonal performance.

Have the class read several psalms aloud, using different types of performance. The psalms excerpted in the text may be used, and the following are also recommended:

direct:	Psalm 137:1–6
responsorial:	Psalm 148
antiphonal:	Psalm 33:1–8

MUSIC FOR STUDY

Yemenite Cantillation for Prophetic Lesson

Style features

The rhythm of the cantillation is unmetered. The melodic range is c'-f'. The melody is constructed as a series of phrases all consisting of decorations of d'. Melismas provide a sort of musical punctuation within the generally syllabic context. The pitch patterns are modal.

The phrases are adapted for reading text lines of varying lengths.

Score

AM 20, *Hebrew Music,* ed. Eric Werner (Cologne: Arno Volk Verlag, 1961), 37.

John of Damascus (ca. 675–ca. 749), "Golden Kanon" for Easter Day

Style features

Byzantine notation includes indications of dynamic inflection. The rhythm of the kanon is unmetered. The melodic range is d-d'. The melody centers on a. Musical phrases are based on those of the Greek text. The piece is in echos 1.

The entire kanon consists of 8 odes (the second ode appears only in kanones for the season of Lent).

Score

AM 13, *The Music of the Byzantine Church,* ed. Egon Wellesz (Cologne: Arno Volk Verlag, 1959), 19–22.

Recording

Treasures of Byzantine Music. The Byzantine Chorale, Frank Desby, dir. Byzantine Society Records No. 10001. (ode 9 only)

Verse "Eructavit cor meum" from Gradual "Speciosus forma"

Style features

This example facilitates comparison of the Ambrosian version of the Gradual verse with the simpler setting in the *Liber usualis.* Although the general contours of the melody are somewhat similar, the Ambrosian setting is more florid and exploits a slightly wider range.

Score

HAM 1, 11

Recording

HEM nos. 6, 7

SAMPLE TEST QUESTIONS

Multiple Choice

1. Religious toleration of Christianity began as a consequence of the
    _____.

    A. death of Jesus
    B. *Confessions* of St. Augustine
    C. Edict of Milan
    D. Code of Justinian
    E. kontakion

2. A psalm verse is characteristically divided into_____parts.

    A. 2
    B. 3
    C. 4
    D. 8
    E. 23

3. A song based on a biblical text but not taken from the book of Psalms
    is called a(n)_____.

    A. scripture
    B. responsorial
    C. canticle
    D. hymn
    E. echos

4. In a(n)_____ performance, sections of a musical work are
    sung by two groups of singers in alternation.

    A. antiphonal
    B. Byzantine
    C. Celtic
    D. direct
    E. echos

5. When a musical performance is divided between sections sung by a
    soloist and sections sung by a group, the performance is called
    _____.

    A. antiphonal
    B. kanon
    C. responsorial
    D. direct
    E. modal

6. The_____was the most sophisticated musical practice among the branches of the early Christian church.

   A. Ambrosian
   B. Byzantine
   C. Celtic
   D. Mozarabic
   E. Old Roman

7. The Frankish church music tradition is also called _____.

   A. Ambrosian
   B. Jewish
   C. Gallican
   D. Dorian
   E. echos

8. The Christian musical tradition based in _____took its name from one of the great saints of the church, who was once bishop there.

   A. Constantinople
   B. France
   C. Ireland
   D. Milan
   E. Rome

9. Byzantine chant employs a set of eight _____or modes.

   A. canticles
   B. kontakion
   C. tetrachords
   D. octaves
   E. echoi

10. A Byzantine kanon was a type of _____.

   A. hymn based on canticles
   B. musical instrument
   C. instruction to performers
   D. round
   E. tetrachord

True-False/Justification

1. St. Augustine was important to the music of the early church because he permitted the free practice of Christianity.

2. An important feature of the Christian religion and its influence on culture is its dependence on literacy.

3. Early Christian worship and music were derived from the practices of the ancient Greeks.

4. Jewish thought about music included a concept of musical ethos or the therapeutic value of music.

5. All the music of the early church was based on texts taken from scripture.

6. The conceptual basis of musical structures in Judaeo-Christian musical tradition differed from that of the Greeks and Romans.

7. Jewish and early Christian music never employed instruments.

8. A kontakion was a point of contact between different musical cultures in the centuries between 300 and 800.

9. The early Christian music and musical practice of Spain is known as Mozarabic.

10. None of the diverse Christian musical repertoires of the early Middle Ages was preserved in musical notation.

Short Essay

Compare St. Augustine's theological position regarding music and religion to Aristotle's views of musical ethos.

ANSWERS TO SAMPLE TEST QUESTIONS

Multiple Choice

1. C   Edict of Milan
2. A   2
3. C   canticle
4. A   antiphonal
5. C   responsorial
6. B   Byzantine
7. C   Gallican
8. D   Milan
9. E   echoi
10. A   hymn based on canticles

True-False/Justification

1. F   Augustine's important contribution to church music was his articulation of theological issues regarding music and religious faith.

2. T Christianity is based on written scriptures, and this also supported the church's position as custodian of culture.

3. F Christian music came from that of the Jews.

4. T The Old Testament story of King Saul and David is an example of this.

5. F Hymns do not come from the Bible.

6. T Jewish and early Christian music was based on melodic formulas or modes.

7. F There are numerous biblical references to the use of instruments in religious music.

8. F A kontakion was an extensive sacred song in Byzantine church music.

9. T Christians in Spain during the period of Moorish domination were called Mozarabs.

10. F The Old Roman and Ambrosian, and to a lesser extent the Gallican and Mozarabic, repertoires were notated.

CHAPTER 3

THE CHANT OF THE MEDIEVAL CHURCH

CHAPTER OVERVIEW

The chant practice of the Catholic Church began to be unified at about the time of the formation of the Holy Roman Empire. The music was conceived and must be understood within the context of the elaborate liturgy of the Divine Office and the Mass. The Office, stabilized first, was intended for worship in the religious community and focused on the singing of psalms, hymns, and canticles. The Mass, which featured the celebration of the Eucharist, had a more complex structure.

The style characteristics of the chant correspond to the aesthetic principles underlying it. Different chant styles were also adapted to different types of textual material and different singers .

The music theory of the chant derived from the classification of chants into modes corresponding to the Psalm tones. In order to aid the singers, musicians developed music notation, eventually arriving at staff notation. The solmization system helped singers to learn to read the pitches accurately.

Later outgrowths of the chant repertoire depended on the principle of the gloss or trope. These included the Sequence and the liturgical drama.

OBJECTIVES

1. To acquaint the student with the historical background for the formation of a catholic chant repertoire.

2. To familiarize the student with the fundamental principles and parts of the Roman liturgy.

3. To help the student understand the aesthetic principles on which the chant style is based and the characteristics of that style.

4. To give the student an understanding of the principles of the music theory of the chant, including the modes and the solmization system.

5. To acquaint the student with the later accretions to the chant
    repertoire.

TERMS, NAMES, AND CONCEPTS

chant
Pope Gregory I
schola cantorum
liturgy
liturgical year
St. Benedict
Divine Office
    Greater Hours—Matins, Lauds, Vespers, Compline
    Lesser Hours—Prime, Terce, Sext, None
Breviary, Antiphonary
antiphon
responsory
Magnificat
Nunc dimittis
Mass
    Introit
    Kyrie
    Gloria
    Gradual
    Alleluia
    Credo
    Offertory
    Sanctus
    Agnus dei
    Communion
    Benediction
Gradual, Missal
Liber usualis
Ordinary, Proper
Requiem Mass
recitation tone
Psalm tone
    initium (intonation), tenor, flex, mediatio (mediant),
    terminatio (termination)
centonization
syllabic, melismatic
ecclesiatical modes
    final, dominant, ambitus authentic, plagal
neume
heighted neumes
ligature
Guido of Arezzo
hexachord
solmization
mutation

gamut
trope
prosa
Sequence
Notker Balbulus
Dies irae
Hildegard von Bingen
liturgical drama

CLASSROOM APPROACHES, ASSIGNMENTS, TOPICS FOR DISCUSSION

Liturgy

To make students conscious of the liturgical calendar, have them look up their name days (the feast day of the saint for whom one is named), if possible; alternatively, have them discover on what festival their birthdays fall. Point out the rationale for the British names for the terms of the academic year—Michaelmas, Hilary, and Trinity.

Assign students to collect service bulletins, worship folders, or programs from local churches. Have them identify which worship elements correspond to the liturgical practice of the medieval church. If possible, identify parts of the service that are proper and ordinary. Note that some important elements of typical contemporary American worship come from the Office (e.g., hymns) and some from the Mass (e.g., scripture reading, Holy Communion). Take note of observances of the festivals of the liturgical year, if any.

Encourage students to attend church services, including a Roman Catholic Office and Mass, if possible. Stress the importance of understanding the liturgy through experience and as a participatory worship activity involving visual and movement components, rather than merely as a series of musical pieces taken out of context. Students should examine the church architecture and see how it is related to musical performance (i.e., processional music, singing by soloists and choir, congregational singing).

Show students the sources for the Roman liturgy, at least the *Liber usualis*. Have them look up particular items or major festivals so that they discover how the sources are organized and used.

Musical Style of the Chant

There is no substitute for singing in order to learn the style of the chant. Have students sing examples of chant in class, preferably from square notation. Discuss the main style traits of each type of chant.

Begin by singing or having one student sing a prayer to a recitation tone, to which the class can respond with an "Amen." Note the limited melodic contour and use of simple melodic gestures for punctuation.

Divide the class into halves facing each other across an open space for the antiphonal singing of a psalm. Note the components of the Psalm tone, intonation, tenor, flex, mediant, termination.

Perform a chant hymn in unison. Note the relatively nonvirtuosic style, with primarily syllabic text underlay and strophic form.

Recruit a student to serve as soloist for a responsorial chant. Note the characteristic elaborateness of the melodic style.

Sing a Gloria or Credo in unison (direct performance), with a soloist beginning the chant with "Gloria in excelsis Deo" or "Credo in unum Deum." Note that settings of these movements often start with the phrase following those openings. Have students outline the phrase structure using letter names (a, b, c, a', etc.) in order to observe the traces of construction of these chants by centonization.

Chant Theory and Notation

Have students examine some examples of chant notation. Draw attention to the four-line staff, the C and F clefs, the custos (guide, direct) at the end of the line. Explain the basic principles of reading single notes and compound neumes. (Point out particularly the ligatures indicating upward melodic motion, since students might not instinctively choose to sing two vertically aligned notes from bottom to top.)

Ask students to examine a number of examples of chant to determine their mode. They should proceed systematically by identifying in order (1) the final, (2) the dominant, (3) the ambitus. Begin with straightforward examples, then introduce such problems as transposed modes (e.g., the Gradual for the Easter Mass "Haec dies") or mixed modes (e.g., the Sequence for the Easter Mass "Victimae paschali laudes").

Have students sing a chant using the Guidonian solmization syllables. If they are not used to singing from syllables, they may wish to write the syllables into the music. They should plan ahead to determine where mutations should take place.

Assign students to compose a melody to set a hymn text in chant style. The melody should belong clearly to one of the church modes. Text underlay should be mostly syllabic with possibly a few syllables set to two of three notes. Students should strive for clear phrase shapes and overall design.

MUSIC FOR STUDY

Office of Second Vespers, Nativity of our Lord

Style features

The Office illustrates the singing of psalms and the canticle "Magnificat anima mea Dominum," using Psalm tones and corresponding antiphons. (The antiphon for the Magnificat, "Hodie Christus natus est," may be familiar to students from Benjamin Britten's *Ceremony of Carols*.)

The Responsory "Verbum caro factus est" is a useful example for class performance of a responsorial chant.

The Hymn "Christe redemptor omnium" represents the style clearly. As an example for singing with hexachord solmization, it requires an easy mutation from the natural to the hard hexachord and back.

Score

* NAWM 1, 18–29

Mass for Easter Day

Style features

The Easter Mass provides a complete liturgy, including the Sequence.

Scores

AMM, 7–29. Presents the complete music of the Mass, including the recited portions and lessons, in "modernized" notation.

* EMH, 2 –23 . Gives the musical movements of Proper and Ordinary, including the prosa "Fulgens praeclara" rather than the more common Sequence "Victimae paschali laudes. "

OMM, 28–47. Contains a very detailed, complete version of the Mass according to the practice of the Cathedral at Salisbury (Sarum) . The notation is "modernized. "

SSHS 1, 7–18 . Provides the complete music of the Mass in chant notation, including recitation, except for the lessons .

Recording

Liturgia Paschalis. Choir of the Monks of the Benedictine Abbey of St. Martin, Beuron, Maurus Pfaff, dir. Archiv 3088/90.

Kyrie IV: Cunctipotens and Trope

Style features

Comparison of the untroped and troped forms of the Kyrie shows how the melismatic passage of the former compares to the syllabic Latin glosses on the nouns of address "Kyrie" and "Christe."

The chant is in mode 1, although it does not end on the final.

Scores

   * EMH 5–7

   HAM 1, 13

   SSHS 1, 19–21

Recording

   HEM nos. 12, 13

Hildegard von Bingen, Sequence "De Sancta Maria"

Style features

   Students should notice that the clef shifts from the third to the second line of the staff in the middle of the fourth stanza, in order to accommodate the higher tessitura of the remainder of the music.
   The appearance of a as the last note indicates that the piece employs a transposed mode, but the mode is somewhat unclear (certainly not "Aeolian," as the commentary in the source given here claims). There are suggestions of modes 2 and 1 in the first part, but the bulk of the Sequence seems to belong to mode 4.

Score

   HAMW, 8–9

The Play of Herod (12th century)

Style features

   The drama is connected to the liturgy of Matins.
   Most of the melodies employ mode 1. The "Te Deum laudamus," with which the drama concludes, uses mode 4.
   There is some attempt at musical characterization: The "women" in Scene 1 sing in a high register, in mode 7; the three Magi are distinguished by register at "Ecce stella."

Score

   OMM 47–60

Recording

   The Play of Herod. New York Pro Musica, Noah Greenberg, dir. Decca 10,095/10,096.

SAMPLE TEST QUESTIONS

Multiple Choice

1. The papal choir, which was responsible for the propagation of church music, was called the _____.

   A. Divine Office
   B. schola cantorum
   C. *Liber usualis*
   D. ecclesiastical mode
   E. gamut

2. The establishment of a uniform chant repertoire began under Charlemagne's rule in the _____ century.

   A. fifth
   B. seventh
   C. ninth
   D. tenth
   E. eleventh

3. The prescribed order for the conduct of worship is called the

   _____.

   A. Alleluia
   B. Gradual
   C. liturgy
   D. Rule of St. Benedict
   E. Sequence

4. The music of the seasons of Advent and Lent in the church calendar is more restrained and sober than at other times of the year because these are _____ seasons.

   A. penitential
   B. Pentecostal
   C. solmization
   D. pagan
   E. monastic

5. The parts of a worship service for which the words are always the same are classified as _____.

   A. schola cantorum
   B. Proper
   C. Offertory
   D. Ordinary
   E. trope

6. The *Magnificat* and the *Nunc dimittis* are _____ for Vespers and Compline respectively.

   A. antiphons
   B. Introits
   C. hymns
   D. gospels
   E. canticles

7. A_____is identified by its intonation, tenor, mediant, and termination.

   A. Mass
   B. Kyrie
   C. Psalm tone
   D. recitation tone
   E. mode

8. The eleventh-century music theorist_____ had an important hand in the development of music education for church singers.

   A. St. Benedict
   B. Alcuin
   C. Notker Balbulus
   D. Hildegard von Bingen
   E. Guido of Arezzo

9. The Mass for the Dead is known as the _____ Mass.

   A. Good Friday
   B. Prime
   C. solmization
   D. Dies Irae
   E. Requiem

10. A(n)_____may be defined simply as the addition of words or music or both to an existing chant.

    A. Introit
    B. Kyrie
    C. ambitus
    D. mode
    E. trope

True-False/Justification

1. Pope Gregory I was the composer of the main body of the chant of the medieval Roman church.

2. The liturgical year does not begin on the same day as the secular calendar year.

3. The first of the Divine Offices each day is called Prime.

4. The most solemn service in the Roman liturgy is the Mass.

5. The Alleluia is part of the Ordinary of the Mass.

6. The actual words are not particularly important in the chant, since the main purpose is to establish a generally worshipful ethos.

7. Spatial relationships were an important factor in the music of the medieval church.

8. The medieval church modes consist of eight-note diatonic scales beginning on d, e, f, and g, respectively.

9. Women never participated in church music.

10. The liturgical drama originated when singers began to act out the dialogue-like parts of music for worship services.

Short Essay

Explain how the structure of the Mass is divided into large, clearly articulated divisions, and explain where the climax of each division falls.

Discuss the consequences for musical composition and for music theory of a musical system such as that for the chant, in which the smallest musical units are melodic phrases (rather than isolated notes).

Why did it seem important beginning in the ninth century to maintain the accuracy of authoritative chant practice? What means did musicians invent to help singers perform the music accurately?

ANSWERS TO SAMPLE TEST QUESTIONS

Multiple Choice

1. B   schola cantorum
2. C   ninth
3   C   liturgy
4. A   penitential
5. B   Proper
6. E   canticles
7. C   Psalm tone
8. E   Guido of Arezzo

9. E   Requiem
10. E   trope

True-False/Justification

1. F   Gregory's contributions to church music seem to have been mostly administrative.

2. T   It begins on the fourth Sunday before Christmas.

3. F   Prime is preceded by Matins and Lauds.

4. T   The Mass climaxes in the sacrament of the Eucharist.

5. F   The Alleluia belongs to the Proper of the Mass.

6. F   The words guide the structure of the chant melodies and the church fathers often expressed concern that the words be clearly understood.

7. T   The practice of the liturgy included specific movement and positions of singers in the church.

8. F   A mode is a melodic pattern determined by the final, dominant, and ambitus of a piece.

9. F   Nuns sang the liturgy in convents, and the abbess Hildegard von Bingen was a significant composer.

10. T   The earliest example of the practice consists of staging directions added to the regular liturgy that recounted the Easter story.

CHAPTER 4

MEDIEVAL SECULAR SONG AND INSTRUMENTAL MUSIC

CHAPTER OVERVIEW

Secular music in the early Middle Ages is not well documented. From the eleventh and twelfth centuries musical sources survive for the lighthearted songs of the Goliards, the more serious conductus, and the epic chansons de geste. Secular professional musicians and entertainers were the minstrels or jongleurs.

Secular song composition attained new sophistication in the works of the troubadours of southern France in the twelfth century, and this art passed to the trouveres in northern France and the Minnesinger in Germany. Their lyrics were closely tied to the cultivation of chivalry in the medieval courts. These songs were also important because they explored the possibilities of musical form.

Other regions developed characteristic song styles as well, including the laude in Italy, Geisslerlieder in Germany, cantigas in Spain, and carol in England.

The instruments of the Middle Ages were classified into haut and bas types. Musicians played a wide variety of string, wind, and percussion instruments, as well as the organ. Instrumentation was not specified in medieval scores, but literary and visual evidence shows that instruments were used to accompany singers and dancing.

OBJECTIVES

1. To give the student an understanding of the place of secular song and instrumental music in medieval musical culture.

2 To acquaint the student with the various repertoires of medieval secular music.

3. To help the student understand the content and style of troubadour, trouvere, and Minnesinger songs.

4. To familiarize the student with the instruments of the Middle Ages and their uses.

TERMS, NAMES, AND CONCEPTS

Goliards
Carmina Burana
conductus
planctus
chanson de geste
minstrel, jongleur
troubadour, trouvère
canso, chanson
    planh
    tenso, descort
    pastorela, pastourelle
    alba, aubade
    balada, ballade
frons, pes, cauda
Minnesinger
Minnelied
Bar
    Stollen
    Abgesang
Meistersinger
lauda
Geisslerlied
Cantigas de Santa Maria
carol
burden
haut, bas
harp
psaltery, canon
lute
rebec
vielle, Fiedel
hurdy-gurdy, organistrum
recorder
transverse flute
shawm
bagpipes
kettledrum, naker
pipe and tabor
positive organ
portative organ
estampie
punctus
ouvert, aperto; clos, chiuso

CLASSROOM APPROACHES, ASSIGNMENTS, TOPICS FOR DISCUSSION

Medieval Secular Song

Have the students listen in class to Carl Orff's *Carmina Burana*. Discuss the style of the settings. In what ways does the music imitate the actual style of medieval music? How effectively did Orff capture the spirit of the lyrics?

Assign students to compose a song (lyrics for an existing melody, melody for an existing text, or both words and music) modeled on the style of a troubadour song. Have the students perform their songs in class.

Hold a debate in the style of a chivalrous disputation on the question whether it is more seemly for a troubadour to sing his songs for his mistress himself or to engage a minstrel to perform on his behalf. Assign the affirmative position to several women students and the negative to men, or vice versa.

Listen to and analyze a medieval dance song and a current popular dance song. Ask the students to identify resemblances and differences between those songs. Comparison should include the subjects and poetic imagery in the lyrics, musical forms, and ways in which a popular song in either period is suitable for dancing.

Medieval Instruments

If possible, show and demonstrate medieval instruments to the students. Allow them to experiment with the instruments. Discuss which seem appropriate for indoor and outdoor use, which could be combined effectively, and which would be most suitable for accompanying singing.

Assign students to score a medieval secular song or dance (if period instruments are unavailable, any instruments may be used). They should employ the instruments in a variety of functions, including preludes, interludes, and postludes; marking rhythms; drone support; heterophonic texture.

MUSIC FOR STUDY

Bernart de Ventadorn (ca. 1125–ca. 1180), "Can vei la lauzeta mover"

Style features

The song is unmetered, but patterned rhythm has been proposed (see SSHS score).

The eight melodic phrases have considerable variety in shape and pitch goals. Text underlay is mostly syllabic with a few neumatic syllables. The modality is that of ecclesiastical mode 1.

The overall form is strophic. The stanza is somewhat unusual in being entirely through-composed.

Scores

> * EMH, 42–44. This score shows the piece in square notation and clearly illustrates the concept of "neumatic" text underlay.

> OMM, 63–63

> * NAWM 1, 34–35

> SSHS 1, 21–24. The introduction shows a hypothetical metrical reading, and the song is given in five variants.

Countess Beatriz de Dia (d. ca. 1212), "A chantar"

Style features

> The modality is that of ecclesiatical mode 2. The stanza form is clear and simple:

> a b   a b   c d b

Scores

> HAMW, 11–13

> * NAWM 1, 36

Richard Coeur-de-Lion (1157–1199), "Ja nun hons pris"

Style features

> Within its limited range, this melody has a well-planned contour. The first phrase of the cauda presents the single appearance of the highest pitch; the final phrase stresses the lowest pitch. The modality is that of ecclesiastical mode 2, transposed to a. Each "open" phrase cadences on g.
> The three-section structure A (ab) A (ab) B (cd) is very clear. The text reflects Richard's imprisonment as a hostage.

Score

> HAM 1, 16

Recordings

> HEM no. 19a

> *Chansons des Rois et des Princes du Moyen Aqe.* Ensemble Perceval, Guy Robert, dir. Arion ARN 68031 (CD).

Walter von der Vogelweide (ca. 1170–1228), "Nu al'erst lebe ich"

Style features

>   The song has very regular rhythm with duple beat divisions and groupings. The melody is particularly well designed both within each phrase and over the length of the stanza. The modality is that of ecclesiastical mode 1.
>   This song exemplifies the Bar structure.

Scores

>   HAM 1, 18
>
>   SSHS 1, 26

Recording

>   HEM no. 20b

Danse royale (Ductia)

Style features

>   The rhythm in this example is regularly articulated in units of 4 × 3 beats, with three units in each punctus. The modality is that of ecclesiastical mode 1, transposed to g.
>   The example clearly illustrates the use of paired puncta with recurring open and closed endings.

Score

>   HAM 1, 42

Recordings

>   HEM no. 40a. This recording uses modern instruments (viola and bassoon) and can serve to suggest to students that they need not hesitate to try modern instruments for medieval music if period instruments are not available. It might also suggest the value of creative scoring and instrumentation.
>
>   *The Medieval and Renaissance Harp.* Elena Polanska, harp; La Camerata. MMG/Vox Prima MWCD 7146.

SAMPLE TEST QUESTIONS

Multiple Choice

1. The bawdy songs sung by renegade clerical students in the eleventh and twelfth centuries are called _____.

    A. Geisslerlieder
    B. Goliard songs
    C. musica humana
    D. chansons de geste
    E. hurdy-gurdy

2. The epic poems of the early Middle Ages, intended to be sung to melodic formulas, were the _____.

    A. aubades
    B. Bars
    C. chansons de geste
    D. minstrels
    E. Minnesinger

3. A planctus was a medieval _____.

    A. musician and general entertainer
    B. lament
    C. German song in several verses with a refrain
    D. string instrument played with a plectrum
    E. dance form

4. The troubadours worked in the region that today is _____.

    A. northern Italy
    B. western Spain
    C. eastern England
    D. central Germany
    E. southern France

5. The_____ was a type of troubadour song that told of an amorous encounter between a knight and a shepherdess.

    A. planctus
    B. tenso
    C. frons
    D. pastorela
    E. estampie

6. The structural basis of many medieval secular songs was a stanza whose form may be outlined _____.

   A. a a b
   B. a b a
   C. a b a b
   D. a b a c a
   E. a b c b a

7. The principal form of German secular songs in the Middle Ages was the _____.

   A. ballade
   B. Bar
   C. bas
   D. burden
   E. rebec

8. The term _____ was used to characterize medieval instruments that were appropriate for outdoor performance.

   A. aperto
   B. positive
   C. haut
   D. hurdy-gurdy
   E. lauda

9. A small medieval organ that could be carried and played by a single player was called _____.

   A. tenso
   B. pes
   C. transverse
   D. positive
   E. portative

10. Paired segments of music with alternating open and closed endings formed the structural basis of a popular medieval dance, the _____.

    A. estampie
    B. punctus
    C. portative
    D. planctus
    E. pipe and tabor

True-False/Justification

1. As a result of the church's domination of European culture, there was no secular music in the early Middle Ages.

2. The medieval jongleur was a popular entertainer and had a wide variety of skills besides performing music.

3. The songs of trouveres were soon imitated by their successors, the troubadours.

4. Music formed an important component in medieval chivalry.

5. The songs of the Minnesinger were generally inclined to be more sober in their poetic content than those of the trouveres.

6. The courtly entertainment of Spain in the thirteenth century featured songs with partly religious subject matter.

7. The carol was originally a Christmas hymn imported into Europe from Judaea as Christianity spread westward.

8. The musicians of the Middle Ages employed a wide variety of chordophones (string instruments).

9. Musicians in the Middle Ages did not yet understand the concept of half cadences and full cadences.

10. Because they hoped to encourage the growth of the church, the medieval church leaders encouraged the lively participation of instruments in worship.

Short Essay

Give several examples of the difficulties presented by the limitations of written secular music from the Middle Ages. Explain how modern musicians can learn about and recreate this music based on other types of evidence.

Discuss two examples of the effect of the church's pervasive influence on the nature and practice of medieval secular music.

ANSWERS TO SAMPLE TEST QUESTIONS

Multiple Choice

1. B   Goliard songs
2. C   chansons de geste
3. B   lament
4. E   southern France
5. D   pastorela
6. A   a a b
7. B   Bar
8. C   haut

9. E   portative
10. A   estampie

True-False/Justification

1. F   There was undoubtedly secular music in the early medieval period, but no notated examples have survived.

2. T   Some of those skills were acrobatics, juggling, and animal training.

3. F   The troubadours appeared first, the the trouveres.

4. T   The songs of the troubadours, trouveres, and Minnesinger were part of the practice of chivalrous love, and their texts explore many approaches to chivalry.

5. T   Many Minnesinger texts are explicitly religious in character.

6. T   The Cantigas de Santa Maria, composed for court use, express devotion to the Virgin Mary.

7. F   The carol was a medieval dance song with a refrain.

8. T   Medieval chordophones included the rebec, vielle, lute, harp, psaltery, and hurdy-gurdy.

9. F   The open and closed endings in many medieval songs and dances employ the half cadence/full cadence contrast.

10. F   The church tended to discourage instrumental music because of its association with pagan activities.

CHAPTER 5

THE DEVELOPMENT OF POLYPHONY

CHAPTER OVERVIEW

The invention of polyphony was the most important musical achievement of the early Middle Ages. The earliest polyphony, parallel, note-against-note organum, dates from the Carolingian era. Also dating from the tenth century is oblique motion in organum.

In the eleventh and twelfth centuries musicians developed melodic independence and rhythmic differentiation between the cantus firmus and second voice in organum. These styles arose contemporary with Romanesque art and architecture.

At Notre Dame in Paris the French Gothic movement, with its emphasis on ordering and organization, produced a system of rhythmic notation to define the previously unmeasured relationships between polyphonic voices. The system of rhythmic modes derived from the meters of Latin poetry. The modes were indicated by ligature patterns. Within the Leonin's style the melismatic type of organum was contrasted with sections in discant style, as the tenor also became measured. Perotin explored three- and four-part textures.

Addition of texts to the upper parts of discant clausulae led to the formation of the motet in the thirteenth century. The resulting syllabic text underlay in turn led to the need for a new kind of rhythmic notation, based on individual note shapes, worked out by Franco of Cologne.

The expressive value of medieval polyphony stems from its symbolic reflection of the rule of number in the order of the universe. Thus the style of the music embodies the principles by which music was placed among the disciplines of the quadrivium, relates the different classifications of music in Boethius's scheme, and mirrors the divine order of nature.

OBJECTIVES

1. To enable the student understand the principle of polyphonic composition based on the chant as preexisting material.

2. To help the student to relate polyphonic musical styles to their contemporary art and thought from the tenth to the thirteenth centuries.

3. To give the student an understanding of the steps in the technical development of polyphony from parallel organum to the late-thirteenth-century motet.

4. To help the student understand the symbolic nature of musical meaning in the Middle Ages.

TERMS, NAMES, AND CONCEPTS

Carolingian era
organum
cantus firmus
parallel organum
    Musica enchiriadis
    Scolica enchiriadis
vox principalis, vox organalis
"free" organum
    Ad organum faciendum
    Winchester Troper
duplum, tenor
Romanesque
melismatic organum, florid organum
discant
Gothic
scholasticism
Leonin
Magnus liber organi
rhythmic modes
long, breve
extensio modi, fractio modi
ordo
clausula
Perotin
organum triplum, organum quadruplum
voice exchange
substitute clausula
contrapuntal cadence
motet
motetus
conductus
cauda
conductus motet
Pierre de la Croix
Franco of Cologne
Ars cantus mensurabilis
tempus
perfection
dot of division
choirbook notation
hocket

CLASSROOM APPROACHES, ASSIGNMENTS, TOPICS FOR DISCUSSION

Artistic and Cultural Movements

Using slides or photographs and plans, compare examples of Carolingian, Romanesque, and Gothic church architecture. Discuss the attributes that the architecture shares with polyphonic music. Students should identify the cruciform foundation, the building up of the structures in layers, the rhythmic differentiation between levels, the symbolic use of numerical proportions.

Assign students to read about the organization and daily routine of the medieval university college. In class discussion, compare the medieval approach to study and the student's life to that of the modern college. Students should consider that some medieval scholars' thoughts are preserved not because they published books but because their students took thorough and excellent notes from brilliant formal lectures. Students are often fascinated by the academic garb, both its practical purposes in the Middle Ages and its symbolism. Discussion should consider what sort of music study belonged to the medieval curriculum and where musicians learned performance skills.

Organum

Point out to students that organum was largely improvisational. Have the students sing a segment of chant in octaves, then in parallel organum at the fifth, then in as many as five parts. Discuss the different effects that result. Does the singing of parallel organum present any difficulties that do not arise in singing in unison or octaves? Have the students sing an example of organum using oblique motion between the parts. In what ways do they find the effect of this procedure differs from that of purely parallel organum? Continue with an example of melodically free organum. Discuss the difficulties of improvising and of choral performance in this style.

Assign students to compose a setting in the style of unmeasured melismatic organum, giving them a section of a responsorial chant to use as cantus firmus. Have them perform the setting in class and discuss the difficulties of coordinating the lines. Next assign a composition using the rhythmic modes (with or without *extensio* and *fractio modi*), including at least one passage of long, unmeasured tenor notes as well as at least one passage in discant style. It is more practical for students to work in two voices (cantus firmus and one added part) than more. They should perform their work in class, scoring the performance in a suitable and imaginative way. They might consider an appropriate sustaining instrument for the sustained tenor notes, and percussion to mark the units of the rhythmic modes or ordines .

Motet

Assign students to write (in English) motet text(s) based on a two- or three-part Notre Dame discant clausula. Alternatively, they might employ a clausula they composed for one of the assignments above. The text(s) should fit the rhythm and phrasing of the existing duplum (and triplum) and form a gloss of the tenor 's text.

MUSIC FOR STUDY

Parallel organum, "Sit gloria Domini" from Musica enchiriadis

Style features

The melodic and rhythmic style retain the character of the chant. Both the vox principalis and vox organalis are doubled at the octave, producing four parts. The resultant harmonic intervals are exclusively fourths, fifths, and octaves.

Scores

HAM 1, 22

OMM, 84

Recording

HEM no. 25b

"Rex caeli, Domine" and "Te humilis famuli" from Musica enchiriadis

Style features

Melody and rhythm retain the character of chant. Oblique motion between voices produces intervals of seconds and thirds as well as fourths. The unison is arrived at before the conclusion of the example, so that there is no true contrapuntal cadence.

Scores

AAM, 18

HAM 1, 22

* MM, 16–17

OMM, 84

Recording

HEM no. 25b

Free organum "Cunctipotens genitor" from Ad organum faciendum

Style features

Solo scoring is clearly more practical than choral performance by this stage.

Harmonic intervals are almost exclusively perfect. Contrary motion predominates. Contrapuntal cadences are created by contrary motion in 5-8 (fifth-to-octave) or 4-1 (fourth-to-unison) progressions.

Scores

HAM 1, 22

SSHS 1, 27

Recording

HEM no. 26a

Melismatic organum "Cunctipotens genitor" from Codex Calixtinus

Style features

Rapid motion in the organal voice contrasts to significantly slower motion in the principal voice. Rhythm is still unmeasured and voices must be coordinated by eye and ear.

The upper voice is extremely florid and reaches an unusually high register. The two voices are strongly distinguished by their contrasting melodic styles. All the intervals from unison to eleventh are used. The contrapuntal cadences take variety of forms; the final cadence illustrates the 3-1 (third-to-unison) type.

Scores

* EMH, 55–56

HAM 1, 23

Recording

HEM no. 27b

Notre Dame organum, discant, and motets on "Haec dies . . ."

Style features

The example incorporates a set of materials for the Gradual of the Easter Mass, as follows:

Two-voice Notre Dame organum in the style of Leonin, illustrating discant clausulae (Domino and In seculum) and modal rhythm. The choral portions of the Gradual remain in unison chant; only the solo portions are set polyphonically.

A set of substitute clausulae for "Haec dies."

A three-voice setting in the style of Perotin.

Motets based on the tenors "Haec dies," Domino," and "In seculum." Note that several of the motetus and triplum voices gloss the Easter text; in the case of the secular texts, this applies in the use of poetic references to the Spring season.

Score

* EMH, 83–87 gives additional materials.

HAM 1, 27–35

Recording

HEM nos. 29–32e

Note: The equivalent material for the "Alleluia Pascha nostrum" provides another fine set of examples. Scores are available in EMH, 58–74 (with EMH recordings); NAWM 1, 47–57 (with NAWM recordings); SSHS 1, 27–34.

Notre Dame conductus "Deus in adjutorium"

Style features

The rhythmic and melodic style of all three voices is similar. Rhythmic caesuras occur simultaneously in the three parts. The cadences of the second, third, and fourth phrases illustrate the $\frac{6}{3}-\frac{8}{5}$ type. This conductus is strophic in four stanzas. The example is *sine cauda*.

Scores

* EMH, 74–75

OMM, 112

"Pucelete/Je languis/Domino"

Style features

This motet shows the differentiation of voices by rhythm; the triplum employs rhythms based on rhythmic mode 6, the motetus employs rhythms of mode 2, and the tenor moves in mode 5.

The phrasing of the three lines is staggered so that caesuras do not generally take place in all voices simultaneously.

Scores

HAM 1, 26

* NAWM 1, 72–74

Recordings

HEM no. 28h

The Medieval and Renaissance Harp. Elena Polanska, harp; La Camerata. MMG/Vox Prima MWCD 7146. This performance is scored for medieval harp, lute, and recorder without voices.

"Je cuidioe/Se j'ai folement aimé/Solem"

Style features

The motet illustrates the free and rapid triplum rhythms associated with the style of Pierre de la Croix. The three voices are clearly differentiated by the use of contrasting predominant rhythmic values. The upper parts proceed freely over three statements of the tenor. This example also shows the use of hocket.

The final cadence is a variant of the $\frac{6}{3}-\frac{8}{5}$ progression, $\frac{10}{6} - \frac{12}{8}$.

Scores

HAM 1, 38–39

SSHS 1, 41–43

Recording

HEM no. 35

SAMPLE TEST QUESTIONS

Multiple Choice

1. The earliest surviving treatises and examples of polyphonic music date from the _____ century.

   A. ninth
   B. tenth
   C. eleventh
   D. twelfth
   E. thirteenth

2. The chant melody that served as the foundation for a medieval polyphonic composition is commonly called its _____.

    A. cantus firmus
    B. vox organalis
    C. discant
    D. conductus
    E. perfection

3. The musical style _____is associated with the abbey of St. Martial in France and the cathedral of Santiago de Compostela.

    A. parallel organum
    B. free organum
    C. melismatic organum
    D. substitute clausula
    E. motet

4. The first composer of polyphonic music whose name we know was _____.

    A. Romanesque
    B. Franco of Cologne
    C. Leonin
    D. Perotin
    E. Pierre de la Croix

5. The system of rhythmic modes is illustrated in music contained in _____

    A. *Musica enchiriadis*
    B. *Winchester Troper*
    C. *Summa theologica*
    D. *Magnus liber organi*
    E. *Ars cantus mensurabilis*

6. One of the important contributions of _____ was the composition of polyphonic pieces in three and four parts.

    A. Winchester Troper
    B. Notker Balbulus
    C. Leonin
    D. Perotin
    E. Thomas Aquinas

7. The addition of words to untexted lines of a polyphonic clausula produced the thirteenth-century _____.

    A. vox principalis
    B. conductus
    C. tenor

D. trope

E. motet

8. A_____was a melismatic elaboration preceding the close of a piece of syllabic polyphony.

A. cauda

B. clausula

C. cadenza

D. discant

E. voice exchange

9. The late-thirteenth-century theorist _____ developed a method of notating rhythm using single notes with dots to indicate beat groupings.

A. Winchester Troper

B. St. Martial

C. Leonin

D. Perotin

E. Franco of Cologne

10. The breaking up of a musical line between two voices by having them alternate notes and rests produces the effect called

_____.

A. discant

B. fractio modi

C. dot of division

D. hocket

E. substitute clausula

True-False/Justification

1. The development of polyphony allowed increased rhythmic and melodic freedom in music.

2. The basis for the composition of organum was the same as that of the trope in the chant.

3. The Romanesque aesthetic in music produced the polyphonic conductus and motet.

4. The cultural center of the development of Gothic style and thinking was Paris.

5. To create a technique for measuring musical rhythm, composers around 1200 turned to their knowledge of mathematics.

6. Once established in a piece of Notre Dame organum the rhythmic mode could not be altered.

7. The basis for a cadence in medieval polyphony was contrary motion.

8. All polyphonic music in the thirteenth century was sacred.

9. As a by-product of Franconian music notation, musicians found a way to save parchment.

10. Because of its sacred and mathematical foundations, medieval music is not expressive.

Short Essay

Explain the steps by which polyphonic composition evolved from early-twelfth-century organum to the motet.

Discuss ways in which polyphonic music in the Middle Ages reflected the authority and intellectual influence of the church.

ANSWERS TO SAMPLE TEST QUESTIONS

Multiple Choice

1. A   ninth
2. A   cantus firmus
3. C   melismatic organum
4. C   Leonin
5. D   Magnus liber organi
6. D   Perotin
7. E   motet
8. A   cauda
9. E   Franco of Cologne
10. D   hocket

True-False/Justification

1. F   The coordination of melodic lines permits less freedom than in monophonic music.

2. T   Both trope and organum consisted of additions to the existing music of the chant.

3. F   Romanesque polyphony included free and florid organum.

4. T   Paris had a leading university as well as the most important school of composition at the church of Notre Dame.

5. F   The rhythmic modes were derived from classical poetic meters.

6. F   The mode could change or be varied by extensio or fractio modi.

7. T   The standard cadential progression was two voices converging from a third to a unison or two voices a sixth apart diverging to an octave.

8. F   Many motets employed secular texts in their upper voices.

9. T   Franco's system for notation allowed the writing of polyphonic music in choirbook notation rather than in score.

10. F   Medieval polyphony expresses symbolically the beauty of order and proportion.

CHAPTER 6

MUSIC IN THE LATE MIDDLE AGES

CHAPTER OVERVIEW

During the fourteenth century political, ecclesiastical, and natural events undermined the dominance of the church over culture and the arts, leading to a shift in interest toward secular affairs. Literary masterpieces in vernacular languages appeared, and musicians, too, worked in genres and styles that increasingly departed from church traditions.

The French music of the fourteenth century is called "ars nova," after the important treatise on rhythmic measurement in the music of the time. The decisive change in rhythmic thinking was the elevation of duple groupings and divisions to equality with triple ones. Rhythm also structured large-scale works in motet style through the process of isorhythm. French secular song developed the forms of troubadour and trouvere lyrics into sophisticated fixed forms. The contrapuntal cadence forms gained strength from the chromatic alteration of the modal seventh (and fourth) to create the leading tone.

A major source of early ars nova music is the *Roman de Fauvel*. The major composers of the first half of the century were Philippe de Vitry and Guillaume de Machaut. In the later part of the century the mannerist style called *ars subtilior* developed.

The fourteenth century in Italy is known as the *trecento*. Italian trecento polyphony was restricted to secular genres. The most distinctive types were the madrigal, ballata, and caccia. Francesco Landini was the leading composer of this period.

England produced characteristic genres and style traits in music at this time. The most important aspect of English style was pervasive use of imperfect consonances, featured in the technique of English discant and also illustrated by the famous *rota* "Sumer is icumen in."

OBJECTIVES

1. To help the student understand the context of cultural crisis and increasing secularism that surrounded the music of the fourteenth century.

2. To introduce the student to the ars nova's innovations in rhythmic notation and style.

3. To familiarize the student with the new elements of musical style in the fourteenth century, including isorhythm, cadence treatment, the forms for French and Italian secular song, and the English style.

4. To give the student an understanding of the concept of mannerism in the history of artistic or musical style.

TERMS, NAMES, AND CONCEPTS

Philippe de Vitry
Ars nova
ars nova, ars antiqua
mensuration, mensuration signature
    tempus
    prolation
isorhythm
    talea
    color
Roman de Fauvel
formes fixes
    ballade
    virelai
    rondeau
double leading-tone cadence
musica ficta
escape-tone cadence
Guillaume de Machaut
Messe de Notre Dame
plainsong Mass
contratenor
mannerism
ars subtilior
trecento
Squarcialupi Codex
Francesco Landini
madrigal
ritornello
ballata
cantilena
ripresa
piedi
volta
caccia, chace
rondellus
pes
gymel
English discant
rota

CLASSROOM APPROACHES, ASSIGNMENTS, TOPICS FOR DISCUSSION

Secularization of Culture

Read in class the descriptions of the Monk and the Friar from the Prologue to Chaucer's *Canterbury Tales*, or one of the stories of lecherous holy men from Boccaccio's *Decameron* (third day, tenth tale; fourth day, second tale). Discuss these examples as symbols of the decadence that existed within the church and instances of the willingness of authors to satirize their spiritual leaders. Compare some of the motet texts of the *Roman de Fauvel* (for an example, see Gustave Reese, *Music in the Middle Ages* [New York: Norton, 1940], 334–335).

Mensural Rhythm

Demonstrate the effect of the mensural signatures on a rhythmic pattern by notating simple series of note values (in longs, breves, semibreves, and minims) and then reading under each of the four basic mensuration signs. (A sophisticated example, dating from the next century, is the second Kyrie from Ockeghem's Missa prolationum, which applies that procedure in an actual piece of music. The original notation may be a challenge for students, since it employs coloration and ligatures "with opposite propriety.")

Ask students to transcribe simple rhythms in modern notation with key signatures of $\frac{9}{8}$, $\frac{3}{4}$, $\frac{6}{8}$, and $\frac{2}{4}$ into mensural notation. It is best to work with rhythms that begin on the first beat of a measure.

Isorhythm

Have students write (in modern notation) a talea of durations of notes and rests, making up from five to ten measures. Then have them compose a melodic pattern or select a passage of chant with a number of notes different from the number of notes in the talea. Finally, have them combine their color and talea to create an isorhythmic line of music. They should explain how many repetitions of color and talea must occur before the line begins to repeat itself (i.e., based on the lowest common multiple of the number of notes in the color and talea). Encourage them to use their imaginations to create isorhythms that explore the possibilities of symbolically important numbers such as 3, 4, 7, 12 or to employ palindromic rhythms.

Forms in Secular Music—French and Italian

As a special project, assign students to write a song in rondeau form. In composing the text they must note that the first line of the refrain (A) and the first two lines of the verse (a, a) will have different words but the same rhythmic structure. The first refrain line (A) must be usable between the first two lines of the verse (i.e., . . . a A a . . .); one way to do this is to open the poem with a phrase of address. The second refrain line (B) and third verse line (b) must have the same rhythmic structure and different words, and each should conclude a thought. In constructing the music, only two phrases need to be composed, the second (B and b) ending with a complete cadence.

Outline for comparison the French ballade form and the Italian fourteenth-century madrigal form, then the French virelai and the Italian ballata. Discuss both the similarities and differences. Be sure that students are clear that ballade and ballata are *not* a similar pair.

Cadences

Trace the development of contrapuntal cadences from the two-voice 6-8 cadence through the addition of the inner voice ($\frac{6}{3} - \frac{8}{5}$ cadence) to the leading-tone and double-leading tone alternations and the addition of the escape-tone ornament. Notate the complete series of five cadence patterns on d; then have students notate them on g.

English Polyphony

Teach students to sing (and/or play on any available instruments) "Sumer is icumen in" (score included in HAM 1, 44–45 and SSHS 1, 44–45). Students should notice the characteristic sound of English harmony, the strength of the melodic phrases, and the use of canonic imitation.

MUSIC FOR STUDY

Philippe de Vitry (1291–1361), "Garrit Gallus/In nova fert/Neuma"

This motet appears in the *Roman de Fauvel*. The text metaphorically attacks the French secular authorities.

Style features

The motet has a partial signature—one flat in the tenor part only. The final cadence is a good example of the three-voice contrapuntal cadence on f, which contains a double leading tone without the application of musica ficta.

The tenor's talea is a palindrome of twelve durations, stated six times. The color has thirty-six pitches, stated twice. The tenor of the second half of the motet is thus identical to that of the first half.

Scores

AMM, 120–126

* NAWM 1, 75–78

Guillaume de Machaut (ca. 1300–1377), "Nes que on porroit"

Style features

Only the topmost line has text; it is possible that the tenor and contratenor were either sung or played on instruments.

Triple compound rhythm is used (perfect tempus and greater prolation).

The piece is based on c and employs both f sharp and b flat, as well as calling for a variety of musica ficta. Both open and closed cadences are employed. (The closed cadences are unusually forward-looking in that the bass moves by fifth under an embellished contrarymotion close in the cantus and contratenor.)

The song is a good example of the three-stanza ballade. The end of the second a-section of the stanza and the end of the refrain are identical.

Score

* EMH, 109–111

Guillaume de Machaut, "Douce dame jolie"

Style features

Duple rhythm is used (imperfect tempus and lesser prolation). The mode is mode 1 transposed to g. The first two sections of the stanza illustrate open and closed endings.

The song is monophonic, in the trouvère tradition. This song is a very concise, clear example of the virelai structure.

Score

SSHS 1, 51–52

Recordings

The Art of Courtly Love. Early Music Consort of London, David Munrow, dir. Seraphim SIC 6092.

The Art of Guillaume de Machaut. Ars antiqua de Paris, Michel Sanvoisin, dir. Musical Heritage Society MHS 3198.

Guillaume de Machaut, *La Messe de Nostre Dame, Chansons.* Boston Camerata, Joel Cohen, dir. Harmonia Mundi HMC 5122.

Guillaume de Machaut, *La Messe de Notre Dame, Chansons.* Various performers, Purcell Choir, Grayston Burgess, dir. Oiseau-Lyre SOL 310.

Guillaume de Machaut, Messe de Notre Dame

The Mass includes the entire Ordinary, with "Ite, missa est."

Style features

    The use of four-part counterpoint gives unusually dense texture for the period.

    The Mass uses the plainsong Mass approach in the shorter movements, adopting the liturgically appropriate chant as tenor. (The Kyrie is based on the Kyrie troped as "Cunctipotens genitor"— see Chapter 3.) The structure is that of the isorhythmic motet, with isorhythm applied in both tenor and contratenor.

Scores

   * MM, 36–39—Agnus Dei 1 only

   * NAWM 1, 87–91—Agnus Dei

   SSHS 1, 45–51—Kyrie, shown in alternatim layout with an organ setting of the chant melody

Recordings (complete Mass)

    Guillaume de Machaut, *La Messe de Nostre Dame, Chansons.* Boston Camerata, Joel Cohen, dir. Harmonia Mundi HMC 5122.

    Guillaume de Machaut, *La Messe de Nostre Dame und Mottetten.* Capella Antiqua Munchen, Konrad Ruhland, dir. Telefunken SAWT 9566.

    Guillaume de Machaut, *La Messe de Notre Dame, Chansons.* Various performers, Purcell Choir, Grayston Burgess, dir. Oiseau-Lyre SOL 310.

    Guillaume de Machaut, *Notre Dame Mass and Gregorian Proper for the Feast of the Assumption.* London Ambrosian Singers and Vienna Renaissance Players, John McCarthy, dir. Nonesuch H 71184. This recording has the advantage of showing how the polyphonic Ordinary fits into the plainchant Proper.

Baude Cordier (fl. ca. 1400), "Belle bonne"

Style features

    The contrasting styles of the parts together with the text in the cantus only suggest performance by solo singer with instrumental tenor and contratenor. Noteworthy is the clear but fleeting contrapuntal imitation at the opening.

Constantly changing rhythm patterns show the possibilities of the mensural system.

The form is that of the rondeau. Cadences at the ends of both musical segments are escape-tone cadences, with single or double leading tones by the application of musica ficta.

Score

HAM 1, 51–52

Recording

HEM no. 48b

Francesco Landini (ca. 1325–97), "Questa fanciull'amor"

Style features

The example shows the structure of the ballata.
Identical escape-tone cadences are used for both musical segments.

Scores

AMM, 162–164

EMH, 122–124

Recordings

Francesco Landini, *Ballate, madrigale, caccia*. Hortus musicus, Andres Mustonen, dir. Melodia 249 002.

Jacopo da Bologna (fl. ca. 1350), "Non al suo amante"

This madrigal's text is by Petrarch.

Style features

The piece clearly calls for two solo singers. The melodic style is extremely florid, a characteristic of Italian taste.

The piece is a typical fourteenth-century madrigal. Cadences are embellished 3-1 patterns. The change of rhythm at the ritornello is characteristic of the fourteenth-century madrigal.

Scores

* EMH, 116–118

HAM 1, 52–53

Recording

HEM no. 49

Gherardello da Firenze, "Tosto che l'alba"

Style features

The caccia consists of two canonic upper parts for singers and an untexted tenor part. The piece concludes with a ritornello, in the manner of a madrigal.
The cadence structures are somewhat unusual.

Scores

* EMH, 118–121

HAM 1, 55–56

SSHS 1, 56–58

Recording

HEM no. 52

SAMPLE TEST QUESTIONS

Multiple Choice

1. The musical style period of the fourteenth century in France is referred to as _____, after an important treatise on music theory.

    A. ars antiqua
    B. ars nova
    C. *Decameron*
    D. Fauvel
    E. musica ficta

2. The rhythmic system invented in the fourteenth century, which employed rhythmic signatures to govern the interpretation of note values, is called _____.

    A. isorhythm
    B. color
    C. mensuration
    D. musica ficta
    E. talea

3. The smallest rhythmic relationship identified by a time signature, that between semibreve and minim, is called _____.

   A. mode
   B. tempus
   C. prolation
   D. mensuration
   E. talea

4. The device known as _____ grew out of the repetitive ordo rhythms in thirteenth-century motet tenors and gave unity to larger and more complex polyphonic pieces in the fourteenth century.

   A. ars antiqua
   B. ars nova
   C. formes fixes
   D. isorhythm
   E. rota

5. One of the most important sources of French early-fourteenth-century music is the _____.

   A. *Ars nova*
   B. *Decameron*
   C. Great Schism
   D. *Roman de Fauvel*
   E. *Squarcialupi Codex*

6. Unlike the ballade and the virelai, the rondeau had _____ stanza(s).

   A. 1
   B. 2
   C. 3
   D. 5
   E. 8

7. Alternations in the regular pitches of the modes in the late Middle Ages, made in order to avoid tritones or to strengthen cadences, were called _____.

   A. color
   B. escape-tone
   C. musica ficta
   D. musica instrumentalis
   E. rota

8. The earliest surviving setting of the complete polyphonic Mass
    Ordinary by a single composer was composed by _____.

    A. Baude Cordier
    B. Jan Hus
    C. Francesco Landini
    D. Guillaume de Machaut
    E. Philippe de Vitry

9. The musical style period of the fourteenth century in Italy is
    referred to as _____.

    A. ars nova
    B. ballata
    C. cantilena
    D. ritornello
    E. trecento

10. The_____was a piece that described outdoor scenes and
    employed canonic imitation between polyphonic voices.

    A. volta
    B. caccia
    C. madrigal
    D. virelai
    E. escape-tone

True-False/Justification

1. In the fourteenth century the authority of the church was
    significantly undermined.

2. Reflecting the increasing secularization of the arts in the
    fourteenth century, the mensural system gave duple rhythms
    precedence over triple ones.

3. Only the composer would normally know of the presence of
    isorhythmic technique in a musical composition.

4. The *Roman de Fauvel* discusses the life of a Roman musician
    studying at the University of Paris in the early fourteenth century.

5. The stanza structure aab is the foundation of each of the three main
    forms in French secular songs of the fourteenth century.

6. Guillaume de Machaut had a varied career as a churchman, court
    official, composer, music theorist, and mathematician.

7. Mannerism is a phenomenon in the history of music and art, in
    which, after the techniques of a style are fully developed, artists
    seem to indulge in the exploitation of technique for its own sake.

8. Italian composers in the fourteenth century did not explore polyphonic styles in sacred music.

9. The Italian ballata was the counterpart of the French ballade, with which it was identical in form.

10. English musicians in the fourteenth century never used the imperfect consonances in their polyphonic music.

Short Essay

Discuss the causes of the changing position of the church in late medieval culture and several evidences of this change in the arts and music.

Why is Machaut's *Messe de Notre Dame* important, and how is it constructed?

ANSWERS TO SAMPLE TEST QUESTIONS

Multiple Choice

1. B   ars nova
2. C   mensuration
3. C   prolation
4. D   isorhythm
5. D   *Roman de Fauvel*
6. A   1
7. C   musica ficta
8. D   Guillaume de Machaut
9. E   trecento
10. B   caccia

True-False/Justification

1. T   Some of the causes of the church's loss of authority were conflict with the secular authorities, abuses within the church, and the Great Schism.

2. F   The mensural system was unbiased toward either duple or triple rhythms.

3. F   The performer of an isorhythmic part would recognize the use of the technique.

4. F   The *Roman de Fauvel* is a series of satiricial stories about an ass named Fauvel, containing many musical pieces.

5. T   The aab stanza form is used in ballade, virelai, and rondeau.

6. F   Machaut was not a theorist and mathematician like Philippe de Vitry, but a poet.

7. T   An example of mannerism is the ars subtilior of late-fourteenth-century French music.

8. T   The Italians concentrated on secular genres.

9. F   The ballata most closely resembles the French virelai.

10. F   The English had a special predilection for thirds and sixths.

CHAPTER 7

THE RISE OF THE RENAISSANCE

CHAPTER OVERVIEW

The general direction of cultural development in Europe in the fifteenth century was determined by a number of causes, including the decline of the church, the rediscovery of ancient thought, new understanding of the world, and the growth of literature. These forces gave rise to the spirit of humanism and marked the beginning of the period of the Renaissance.

The Hundred Years' War brought the English into France, along with their music. The sounds of the English harmony with its emphasis on imperfect consonances appealed to the new generation of composers on the continent. The acknowledged leading composer in this style was the Englishman John Dunstable.

Burgundy maintained a lavish court life and cultivated the arts during this perod. The early development of the new style in continental music was dominated by the Burgundian composers. Most notable among these composers were Guillaume Dufay and Gilles Binchois.

New trends in musical style included not only the adoption of the richer-sounding English harmony, but also the increasing emphasis on four-voice polyphonic textures, the cantus firmus Mass, and cadence forms supported by the skip of a fifth in the bass.

OBJECTIVES

1. To acquaint the student with the nature of the humanist movement and the factors that contributed to it.

2. To give the student an understanding of the ways in which political events influenced the development of music in the fifteenth century.

3. To familiarize the student with the style characteristics of music in the fifteenth century, including the emphasis on imperfect consonances, four-voice texture, the unification of the Mass by a single cantus firmus, new cadence structures.

TERMS, NAMES, AND CONCEPTS

humanism
contenance angloise
panconsonance
John Dunstable
Burgundian school
Guillaume Dufay
superius, contratenor altus, contratenor bassus
fauxbourdon
alternatim
cantus firmus
motto, head motive
Gilles Binchois
octave-leap cadence
authentic cadence

CLASSROOM APPROACHES, ASSIGNMENTS, TOPICS FOR DISCUSSION

Humanism and the Renaissance

In the 1980s secular humanism came under attack from American biblical fundamentalism on the grounds that it represented an abandonment of spiritual values that were upheld by the church. Discuss with the class how this argument would have appeared to Renaissance humanist thinkers. How does the conflict between humanism and the church affect the arts?

Discuss in class the role of books and literacy for the Renaissance. How do students compare the situation with regard to reading and the cultivation of ideas in the fifteenth century to that of modern America? How do they think this might affect music in each of these periods?

Assign the class to read and report on the idea of the "Renaissance man" and such examples as Leon Battista Alberti and Leonardo da Vinci. Could such figures exist in the twentieth century? If so, can the class identify some examples? If not, why not?

New Aspects of Style

Assign students to write a fauxbourdon setting based on a chant hymn melody. The setting should begin and each phrase end on an $\frac{8}{5}$ harmony, with mostly $\frac{6}{3}$ and some $\frac{6}{5}$ harmonies during the phrase. Leading tones may be applied, as well as escape-tone ornaments at cadences.

Demonstrate the development of the contrapuntal cadence in two voices into the octave-leap cadence and then the authentic cadence in four parts using the cadence on g. Have students write out the same series of cadences on d. Point out that the plagal cadence, also employed frequently in the Renaissance, uses parallel (descending thirds or sixths) rather than contrary stepwise motion in two upper voices, combined with bass motion opposite to that of the authentic cadence.

MUSIC FOR STUDY

John Dunstable (ca. 1390–1453), "Veni sancte spiritus/Veni creator spiritus"

Style features

The motet combines the isorhythmic structure and successive proportional diminutions of late medieval French motet construction with the English harmonic style featuring imperfect consonances.

Scores

SSHS 1, 66–69

Recordings

Dufay, Dunstable, *Motets.* Pro Cantione Antiqua, London, Bruno Turner, dir. Archiv 2533 291.

John Dunstable, *Motets.* Hilliard Ensemble, Paul Hillier, dir. Angel D5-38082.

Josquin des Prez, John Dunstable, *Vocal Music.* Purcell Consort of Voices, Elizabethan Consort of Viols, Grayston Burgess, dir. Musical Heritage Society MHS 7244.

John Dunstable, "Quam pulchraes"

Style features

This work is not cantus-firmus-based. The English sonority is extremely clear, and there is a good example of a passage in parallel, discant style.

Scores

* NAWM 1, 99–103

SSMS, 59–61

Guillaume Dufay (ca. 1400–1474), "Christe redemptor omnium"

Style features

Dufay's fauxbourdon setting of his paraphrased version of the Christmas Vespers hymn (see Chapter 3) is arranged for alternatim performance with the simple chant.

Score

* EMH, 143–146

Guillaume Dufay, Missa Se la face ay pale

Style features

The Mass is based on the tenor of Dufay's own chanson, though the use of a contratenor bassus means that the tenor does not have to support the harmonic structure itself. Substantial passages are independent of the chanson. In some cases voices other than the tenor allude to the chanson.

The cadences are remarkable for their arrival on a harmony that includes a third, followed by the abandonment of the third. In Dufay's time the imperfect consonance was still not regarded as suitable for a final cadence.

Scores

* EMH, 146–152– Agnus Dei and tenor of chanson

* MM, 43–47—Kyrie I and tenor of chanson

* NAWM 1, 166–175—chanson and Gloria

SSHS 1, 70–74—Kyrie and Agnus Dei (chanson, p. 117)

Gilles Binchois (ca. 1400–1460), "Deuil angoisseus"

Style features

This ballade-form chanson illustrates the modern harmony of the fifteenth century. The clos ending used for both the second a section and the end of the song provides an example of the octave-leap cadence combined with the escape-tone ornament in the highest part.

Score

OMM, 232–233

Recording

> *The Castle of Fair Welcome.* Gothic Voices, Christopher Page, dir.
> Hyperion CDA66194.

SAMPLE TEST QUESTIONS

Multiple Choice

1. The fifteenth century movement called _____was based
    on the conviction that personal fulfillment could come from the
    intellect and one's own effort.

    A. dogma
    B. empiricism
    C. cosmology
    D. humanism
    E. contenance angloise

2. The reemergence of the works of the Greek philosopher _____
    had an important influence on the thought of the early
    Renaissance.

    A. Pythagoras
    B. Plato
    C. Aristotle
    D. Boethius
    E. Guido

3. An important factor in the spread of new ideas in the Renaissance
    was the invention of _____.

    A. printing from movable type
    B. parchment
    C. music notation based on time signatures
    D. a style of painting free from laws of perspective
    E. Burgundy

4. English musical style spread to the continent of Europe in the early
    Renaissance partly as a consequence of the _____.

    A. Great Schism
    B. Seven Years' War
    C. Thirty Years' War
    D. Hundred Years' War
    E. Council of Constance

5. The leading English composer of the early fifteenth century was
    _____.

    A. Johannes Gutenberg
    B. Pico della Mirandola
    C. Copernicus
    D. Guillaume Dufay
    E. John Dunstable

6. The term "contenance angloise," used to identify a musical style,
    refers to _____.

    A. panconsonant harmony
    B. the octave-leap cadence
    C. the use of a cantus firmus
    D. the Italian approach to melody
    E. contrapuntal lines that diverge at angles

7. _____composed a special motet for the dedication of the
    cathedral dome in Florence, Italy.

    A. Leonardo da Vinci
    B. Leon Battista Alberti
    C. John Dunstable
    D. Filippo Brunelleschi
    E. Guillaume Dufay

8. The creation of_____, derived from English discant,
    involved the composition of a new part below a chant-derived
    melody, and the improvisation of a third line between those two.

    A. head-motive
    B. fauxbourdon
    C. the authentic cadence
    D. virtù
    E. panconsonance

9. The center of musical development in the early fifteenth century
    was_____.

    A. Florence
    B. Burgundy
    C. Paris
    D. England
    E. Rome

10. The early fifteenth-century composer _____was a soldier
    and singer, and he produced mostly secular songs.

    A. Aldus Manutius
    B. Martin le Franc

C. Gilles Binchois
D. John Dunstable
E. Guillaume Dufay

True-False/Justification

1. Even after the reconciliation of the rival factions of the church in 1417 the authority of the church never became as strong as it had once been.

2. An important aspect of the Renaissance was its independence from the authority of ancient classical thought.

3. The Renaissance placed a great deal of value on empiricism and direct observation of the world.

4. The linguistic disciplines were no longer regarded as trivial pursuits in the Renaissance view of thought and study.

5. "Panconsonance" means a musical style based only on the use of perfect consonances.

6. Burgundy became important in fifteenth-century culture because it conquered its neighbors through a series of military campaigns and imposed its artistic tastes throughout a large part of Europe.

7. Guillaume Dufay was an Italian composer who traveled to Burgundy.

8. Because of the special character of sacred music, the melodic line derived from chant was never altered in polyphonic settings in the fifteenth century.

9. "Alternatim" is the term used for the part of the Mass sung by the priest alone, standing before the altar.

10. The use of contrary motion at cadences in polyphonic music was abandoned in favor of the authentic cadence in the fifteenth century.

Short Essay

Explain what international cultural and musical influences converged in France and Burgundy in the fifteenth century and how these fit together to create a new musical style.

Why is a cantus firmus Mass such as Dufay's *Missa Se la face ay pale* evidence of the effect of humanism on Renaissance sacred music?

ANSWERS TO SAMPLE TEST QUESTIONS

Multiple Choice

1. D   humanism
2. B   Plato
3. A   printing from movable type
4. D   Hundred Years' War
5. E   John Dunstable
6. A   panconsonant harmony
7. E   Guillaume Dufay
8. B   fauxbourdon
9. B   Burgundy
10. C   Gilles Binchois

True-False/Justification

1. T   Humanism had grown up to challenge ecclesiastical dogma, so that the church never fully regained its former power.

2. F   Greek and Roman ideas and artistic models became very important to Renaissance thinkers and artists.

3. T   In the Renaissance, empiricism superseded authority and tradition.

4. T   The disciplines of the trivium became much more important in the Renaissance than they had been in the Middle Ages.

5. F   Panconsonance designates a style based on the predominance of imperfect consonances and limited use of dissonance.

6. F   Burgundy's relative peace and wealth allowed the cultivation of the arts.

7. F   Dufay was Burgundian and traveled to Italy

8. F   Many Renaissance settings of sacred music use paraphrases of the liturgical melodies.

9. F   The term "alternatim" refers to the singing of chant and polyphonic passages in alternation.

10. F   The authentic cadence incorporated the contrary motion of the 6-8 cadence.

CHAPTER 8

THE HIGH RENAISSANCE

CHAPTER OVERVIEW

The center of musical development shifted in the late fifteenth century from Burgundy to the large northern and western region called the Netherlands. The leader of the group of composers whose stylistic roots were in the Netherlands was Johannes Ockeghem. His music featured a flowing style and similar melodic character in the various parts. His younger contemporary Jacob Obrecht advanced the new style further.

The acknowledged master composer of the high Renaissance was Josquin des Prez, who created the style called *ars perfecta*. His compositional technique achieved control of harmony, clarity and integration of texture, and responsiveness of the music to the words.

The northern composers spread their style throughout Europe, making it a cosmopolitan musical idiom. It caught on because of its incorporation of the values of humanism and its incorporation of poetic elements into the music. Music also became an important element in secular social life, due to the increase of wealth and education and the availability of affordable printed music.

In the sixteenth century, the different regions of Europe adapted and modified the cosmopolitan northern style, producing distinct idioms associated with the Netherlands, Paris, Germany, and Italy. As the century continued, the most sophisticated work came from Italy, where the madrigal epitomized the modern relation of music to social activity and to literature.

OBJECTIVES

1. To acquaint the student with the development and characteristics of the Franco-Netherlands style.

2. To familiarize the student with the nature of the spread and variation of the northern style.

3. To help the student understand the position of music in social activity in the Renaissance.

4. To give the student a comprehension of the nature, significance, and effect of the use of poetry as the model for musical expression in the Renaissance.

TERMS, NAMES, AND CONCEPTS

"Franco-Netherlands" school
Johannes Ockeghem
canon
Jacob Obrecht
Josquin des Prez
maestro di cappella
Heinrich Isaac
ars perfecta
motet (sixteenth-century style)
fuga
point of imitation f
amiliar style
musica reservata s
oggetto cavato
contrafactum, parody
Lorenzo the Magnificent
Maximilian I
Adrian Willaert
Jean Mouton
St. Mark's basilica
Gioseffe Zarlino
Le istitutioni harmoniche
Ottaviano de Petrucci
Harmonice musices odhecaton A
Pierre Attaingnant
Tylman Susato
Thomas Morley
A Plaine and Easie Introduction to Practicall Musicke
chanson (sixteenth-century styles)
Claudin de Sermisy
Clément Janequin
Meistersinger
Hans Sachs
Lied (polyphonic style)
quodlibet
frottola madrigal
Jacques Arcadelt
Cipriano de Rore

CLASSROOM APPROACHES, ASSIGNMENTS, TOPICS FOR DISCUSSION

Franco-Netherlands Compositional Techniques

Have students examine Ockeghem's *Missa prolationum* and *Missa cuiusvis toni* in class and discover the special technical features of each. Students should discuss in what sense these works seem to look back to the Middle Ages and in what ways they incorporate the ideals of humanism.

Show students how to use the technique of *soggetto cavato* to derive musical ideas from their own names or other words. If their compositional skills are sufficiently advanced, have them compose a fuga passage in three or four voices, using that subject as the point of imitation. If they are less advanced, have them set the subject for four voices in familiar style, first as tenor, then as superius.

Have students list the style characteristics of the fourteenth-century cantus-firmus-based motet and the sixteenth-century motet. Discuss how the change of style reflects changes in values and ideas in European culture and art.

Assign students to create a parody Mass movement based on a secular chanson. They may wish to rearrange the music a great deal or simply to work the Mass movement's text into the notes as they stand. Care should be taken with declamation and punctuation.

Spread of the Northern Style

Assign students to research the careers of some major Renaissance composers, including Josquin des Prez and Heinrich Isaac. On a large map, have students trace the travels of these composers, using a different color for each composer. In each place to which these composers' careers led them, students should indicate whether the composer was employed by the church (marked with a cross or other appropriate symbol) or a court (crown or other symbol) and the dates at which the composer worked there.

Have students report in class on some of the major musical centers or patrons of music in the Renaissance. They might include the general lifestyle of a court or the character of liturgical practice at a church, the types of music that were called for, the composers who worked there, the numbers of players and singers in the musical establishment.

Assign students to compose a quodlibet using familiar songs such as nursery rhymes, folk songs, popular songs, or television commercial jingles. Encourage imagination and humor.

Compare the diffusion of musical style to form a number of regional variant styles in the sixteenth century with the diffusion of Christian music throughout Europe to form regional traditions in the early spread of the church. What similarities and differences are there between these phenomena?

Music for Social Use

If possible, show students a set of part-books for madrigal singing. Have a group of singers perform a madrigal or chanson as chamber music, reading from parts only and sitting around a table. In discussion, ask students to list as many ways as possible how such a performance differs from a choral performance in a concert hall.

Read in class some representative passages of Castiglione's *Il cortegiano*. Discuss what social skills and character traits would be listed if one were to make a modern version of Castiglione's prescription for an upwardly mobile young man or woman. Would music be important in this list and, if so, in what way?

Music and Poetry

Give students a madrigal text without music and have them compose a melodic point of imitation for each line or phrase, responding to both declamation and word meanings. Have them indicate where the text suggests full cadences, transitory or half cadences, elided cadences.

MUSIC FOR STUDY

Johannes Ockeghem (ca. 1420–1496), Missa Mi-Mi, Agnus Dei

Style features

The title of the Mass derives from the cyclic bass motive e (mi in the natural hexachord)/A (mi in the soft hexachord)/e.

The cadences of the first and third sections are plagal cadences, which became the "modern" solution to the handling of the cadences in the E modes. That of the first section clearly incorporates the old-style contrapuntal cadence pattern. The middle section closes in an authentic cadence on g.

The outer sections illustrate Ockeghem's characteristically dense texture in four nearly continuous voices, while the middle section shows thinner (two- and three-part) textures. The style of the different lines is much more homogeneous than that of earlier polyphony.

Scores

* EMH, 161–167. This score includes a facsimile of the original notation.

SSMS, 73–77

Josquin des Prez (ca. 1440–1521), "Ave Maria gratia plena . . . virgo serena"

Style features

This motet is a classic example of the *ars perfecta*. It illustrates the division of the text into periods treated in *fuga*, as paired duets, and in familiar style. A strict canon at the lower fifth appears in the triple-meter section between superius and tenor.

The treatment of the text in each point of imitation is particularly sensitive to the declamation of the words.

Scores

AAM, 58–68

* EMH, 175–182

SSMS, 77–82

Josquin des Prez, Missa Pange lingua

Style features

Another excellent example of Josquin's compositional technique, this Mass is based on points of imitation paraphrased from the melody of the great hymn for Corpus Christi "Pange lingua," the text of which is by Thomas Aquinas.

Scores

AAM, 53–58—Gloria

AMSS, 28–31—Kyrie. Hymn on p. 6.

* EMH, 185–194—Kyrie and Agnus Dei. Hymn on pp. 40–41.

SSHS 1, 80–102—complete Mass with Proper for the Feast of the Nativity of St. John the Baptist by Heinrich Isaac. Hymn on pp. 6–7.

Jean Mouton (ca. 1470–1562), "Noe, noe"
 Jacques Arcadelt (ca. 1505–ca. 1560), Missa Noe, noe, Kyrie and Gloria

Style features

This motet and Mass by two leading Franco-Netherlands composers offer a fine example of the parody technique. Arcadelt's Mass sacrifices the use of text-painting found in Mouton's motet, but it compensates by a more sophisticated working out of the motivic material.

Score

  * NAWM 1, 130–135 and 198–205

Marchetto Cara (ca. 1470–ca.1525), "Io non compro più speranza"

Style features

    The frottola exists in settings for four voices and for solo singer with lute. Generally the texture is homorhythmic (familiar style), with syncopations between the parts providing contrapuntal interest.
    Hemiola appears throughout the piece.
    The form is strophic with a refrain.

Score

  * EMH, 210–212

Claudin de Sermisy (ca. 1490–1562), "Tant que vivray"

Style features

    Duration values are rather strictly determined by French diction, producing simple rhythm and regular movement toward a caesura on the last syllable of each phrase. Familiar style predominates, except at the b section where there is some staggering of phrases among the parts. The top voice clearly carries the melodic interest.
    The vocabulary of harmonies is extremely limited and cadence patterns are fully "modern."
    The song is strophic, each stanza having the form a a b.

Scores

  * NAWM 1, 240–242

  SSHS 1, 122–123

Jacques Arcadelt, "Il bianco e dolce cigno"

Style features

    This famous madrigal is a classic example of the first-generation madrigal style, based on the Franco-Netherlands technique. The rhythms, though ostensibly duple, are flexibly adapted to the declamation of the words. Cadences are principally authentic; the final cadence (meas. 42–43) is extended to a plagal ending (meas. 46). Subtle word-painting is employed, especially in the appearance of the multiple entrances in *fuga* texture at the descending point of imitation for the words "mille morte" (meas. 34ff).

Scores

> * EMH, 263–266

> SSMS, 99–101

Cipriano de Rore (1516–1565), "Da le belle contrade"

Style features

> This madrigal represents the second generation of the genre, with more elaborate vocal parts, more complex textures, more harmonic range, and more vivid depictions of the poetic material in the music. The text is a good example of the post-Petrarchan Italian sonnet.

Scores

> * EMH, 266–271

> HAM 1, 142–143

Anne Boleyn (1507–1536)?, "Oh Deathe, rock me asleepe"

Style features

> The depressed mood of the text is reflected in the descending lines, emphasis on minor thirds, and obsessive repetitions. The final cadence is not a half cadence but a minor plagal cadence.

Score

> HAMW, 14–17

Recording

> *Songs in Shakespeare's Plays.* James Bowman, countertenor; James Tyler, lute. Archiv 2533 407.

SAMPLE TEST QUESTIONS

Multiple Choice

1. The first great composer of the Franco-Netherlands school,
    _____, was a singer, composer, and director at the royal
    court in Paris.

    A. Adrian Willaert
    B. Josquin des Prez
    C. Jacques Arcadelt
    D. Johannes Ockeghem
    E. Jacob Obrecht

2. The term "canon" in fifteenth-century music referred to
    _____.

    A. a musical instrument
    B. an instruction to performers
    C. a round
    D. contrary motion
    E. a French secular song

3. The Renaissance composer whose compositional style was
    considered to embody the "perfect art" was _____.

    A. Johannes Ockeghem
    B. Josquin des Prez
    C. Claudin de Sermisy
    D. Jacques Arcadelt
    E. Gioseffe Zarlino

4. The common term used to designate contrapuntal imitation among
    the voices in a Renaissance composition was _____.

    A. motet
    B. fuga
    C. familiar style
    D. canon
    E. contrafactum

5. The term_____referred to the thoroughgoing
    sensitivity to the relation between words and music.

    A. contrafactum
    B. musica reservata
    C. mimesis
    D. soggetto cavato
    E. quodlibet

6. When a composer borrows a prexisting polyphonic piece, adapting the music to a new text, we say that he produces a _____ of the original work.

   A. soggetto cavato
   B. cancrizans
   C. quodlibet
   D. parody
   E. mimesis

7. _____codified the compositional technique of the high Renaissance in his treatise *Le istitutioni harmoniche.*

   A. Johannes Ockeghem
   B. Josquin des Prez
   C. Adrian Willaert
   D. Gioseffe Zarlino
   E. Cipriano de Rore

8. The first publication of music from movable type dates from _____.

   A. 1470
   B. 1492
   C. 1501
   D. 1521
   E. 1536

9. The_____ characteristically employed the most sophisticated treatment of poetry among the secular genres of the early sixteenth century.

   A. quodlibet
   B. frottola
   C. contrafactum
   D. chanson
   E. madrigal

10. The great Renaissance musicians Willaert, Rore, and Zarlino all worked as music director at _____.

   A. St. Mark's in Venice
   B. St. Peter's in Rome
   C. Notre Dame in Paris
   D. the royal court in Paris
   E. the ducal court in Ferrara

True-False/Justification

1. The cosmopolitan style of music in the high Renaissance was created in Italy.

2. Johannes Ockeghem led in the development of equal-voiced texture.

3. Josquin des Prez's career took him to a number of different cities and included both sacred and secular positions.

4. Because of the humanist influence on Renaissance music, Josquin's Masses never derived material from preexisting sacred music.

5. Adrian Willaert learned his musical style from Zarlino's *Le istitutioni harmoniche*.

6. Although the educated person studied the theory of music, in the sixteenth century, as in the early Middle Ages, musical performance was considered a low-class skill.

7. The Parisian chanson composers of the early sixteenth century paid close attention to the texts they set.

8. English music influenced music on the continent much less in the sixteenth century than in the fifteenth.

9. Because of the dearth of good poetry in Italy after the time of Petrarch, Italian music stagnated throughout the Renaissance.

10. The grammar of a poetic text was an important consideration for Renaissance composers.

Short Essay

Describe the geographic distribution of musical styles in the period 1450–1550, indicating which areas were most prominent during different parts of that century and which seemed to be more peripheral. Explain what extramusical factors directed this development.

Explain several ways in which literature served as a model for musical expression to the composers of the high Renaissance. Cite specific musical examples to illustrate your points.

ANSWERS TO SAMPLE TEST QUESTIONS

Multiple Choice

1. D   Johannes Ockeghem
2. B   an instruction to performers
3. B   Josquin des Prez
4. B   fuga
5. B   musica reservata
6. D   parody
7. D   Gioseffe Zarlino

8. C   1501
9. E   madrigal
10. A   St. Mark's in Venice

True-False/Justification

1. F   The cosmopolitan style stemmed from the north.

2. T   In Ockeghem's more progressive works the various voice parts all employ generally similar melodic style.

3. T   Josquin served churches in Milan, Rome, and the Netherlands, and worked for noble courts in Milan, Ferrara, and possibly Paris.

4. F   Josquin derived material for Masses from both the chant and polyphonic motet repertoire.

5. F   Zarlino's treatise was based on Willaert's style.

6. F   A middle- or upper-class person in the high Renaissance was expected to be able to sing and/or play a part at social gatherings.

7. T   The French composers concentrated on clear and accurate declamation of the poetry.

8. T   England became somewhat more isolated after the end of the Hundred Years' War.

9. F   There was a great deal of excellent Italian poetry in the high Renaissance, which helped produce the brilliant development of the madrigal.

10. T   Grammar directed the lengths of periods and types of cadences used in a polyphonic composition.

CHAPTER 9

INSTRUMENTAL MUSIC IN THE RENAISSANCE

CHAPTER OVERVIEW

In the Renaissance the basic division of instruments into haut and bas types continued from the Middle Ages. In addition, there was a new interest in forming homogeneous ensembles or consorts of matched instruments, resembling vocal choirs. Some of the most common and characteristic consorts were those of recorders, crumhorns, sackbuts, and viols. Broken consorts of contrasting instruments were also possible.

Solo polyphonic instruments included the lute family and keyboard instruments. Music for lutes and for keyboard was notated in tablature, which indicated the placement of fingers rather than presenting a graphic representation of pitch.

Instruments took part in playing Renaissance vocal music, either to double or to replace singers. Some purely instrumental genres were modeled on vocal types, the ricercar on the motet and the canzona on the chanson.

Purely instrumental genres in the Renaissance notably included dances, which frequently came in pairs. In addition, there were sets of variations on either tunes or bass patterns, and pieces written in imitation of improvisations.

OBJECTIVES

1. To acquaint the student with the most important instruments of the Renaissance.

2. To give the student an understanding of the principle of the consort.

3. To help the student understand the principle of tablature.

4. To familiarize the student with the uses of instruments and genres of instrumental music in the Renaissance.

TERMS, NAMES, AND CONCEPTS

chest, consort
crumhorn
schreierpfeife
kortholt
racket
dulcian, curtal
sackbut
cornett, cornetto, Zink
viol, viola da gamba
violone
archlute
    theorbo
    chitarrone
vihuela
broken consort
clavichord
harpsichord
jack
virginal
tablature
ricercar
canzona
In nomine
basse danse, bassadanza
dance pairs
    passamezzo, saltarello
    pavane (pavan), gaillarde (galliard)
variation set
improvisatory pieces
    fantasia
    toccata
    tiento
    intonazione
    prelude, preambulum

CLASSROOM APPROACHES, ASSIGNMENTS, TOPICS FOR DISCUSSION

Renaissance Instruments

If possible, show and demonstrate a variety of Renaissance instruments in class. Encourage students to experiment in playing the instruments themselves. Examine sets of recorders, crumhorns, and viols, noting how the instruments are similar and how alternations in the design are necessary to compensate for size differences. Ask students to compare the Renaissance instruments with modern couterparts. If both haut and bas instruments are available, let students classify them by listening to them.

Discuss the differences in musical effect between ensemble music played with heterogeneous sounds, as in the Middle Ages or a broken consort, and that played with consorts of matched instruments. In what ways do the textures of medieval and Renaissance music suit the heterogeneous and homogenous scorings of their respective periods?

Tablature

Assign students to attempt a transcription of a brief and simple passage in lute tablature (or compare a passage in tablature with a transcription into common notation). Students should observe that the tablature does not easily suggest pitch contours and that the polyphonic texture must be reconstructed in order to show the linear aspect of the music.

Discuss the advantages and disadvantages of tablature and graphic notation of pitch for the string instrument player.

Renaissance Instruments and Vocal Music

Many Renaissance instrumental pieces are suitable for student performance in class. Lute and consort songs can be sung well by young voices. Modern instruments may be used with good effect, even substituting piano for lute (though a harpsichord would be a better stand-in); the difference between the modern instruments and the period ones should be discussed, however.

Renaissance Dance Music

Have students research the choreography of some of the common Renaissance dances, if possible consulting a dance instructor, and then dance some examples in class. Historical accuracy in the students' dancing is commendable, but it is less important than a sympathetic response to the rhythm and phrase structure of the music.

MUSIC FOR STUDY

Adrian Willaert (ca. 1490–1562), Ricercar

Style features

This ricercar in three parts is clearly in vocal style and quite loose in form, showing the features of the contemporary motet. The final cadence is plagal.

Score

HAM 1, 120–121

Florentio Maschera (ca. 1540–ca. 1584), Canzona

Style features

The work illustrates the characteristic opening dactylic rhythm of the genre. The style is generally similar to that of a vocal chanson, but in details seems more idiomatic to instruments.

Score

HAM 1, 201–202

John Dowland (1563–1626), "Flow my teares," and Lachrimae Pavan

Style features

The song is in three repeated sections. The expressive quality derives from descending lines, suspensions, the emphasis on the minor third (c"), and the framing of many phrases by the diminished fourth (g' sharp to c").

The instrumental arrangement of the song by the composer, known as Lachrimae Pavan, links not only vocal to instrumental music but also song to dance.

Scores

* NAWM 1, 333–336, 616–619

SSMS, 124–127

Thomas Tomkins (1573–1656), "In nomine"

Style features

The texture is that of a duet for two viols in idiomatic instrumental style over the cantus firmus "in nomine," also played by viol.

Score

HAM 1, 202–204

Tylman Susato (ca. 1500–ca.1560), Pavane/Gaillarde "Mille ducas"

Style features

This example illustrates the pairing of dances in which the outline of the pavane is reinterpreted in triple meter in the gaillarde. The cadences include a half cadence, authentic cadences, and plagal cadence.

Score

SSMS, 101–102

Luis Milán (ca. 1500–ca. 1561), Fantasia XI for vihuela

Style features

The improvisational-style fantasia is very freely structured in a series of sections in contrasting textures. Its function would have been to introduce another piece in mode 1 or 2.

Score

* NAWM 1, 306–309

SAMPLE TEST QUESTIONS

Multiple Choice

1. A(n) _____ is an ensemble of matched instruments corresponding to the vocal ranges.

    A. haut
    B. racket
    C. intonazione
    D. consort
    E. canzona

2. The _____ has a capped double reed, a cylindrical bore, and a curved design.

    A. chest
    B. crumhorn
    C. sackbut
    D. intonazione
    E. ricercar

3. The virginal was a popular _____ instrument in England in the Renaissance.

    A. woodwind
    B. brass
    C. percussion
    D. string
    E. keyboard

4. The_____ takes its name from the fact that the player holds the instrument between his or her legs.

   A. virginal
   B. theorbo
   C. bassadanza
   D. viola da gamba
   E. fantasia

5. The term_____ could designate either an instrumental work based on the style of the motet or an improvisatory piece.

   A. ricercar
   B. canzona
   C. pavane
   D. dulcian
   E. tablature

6. One of the popular fast dances of the Renaissance was the _____.

   A. preambulum
   B. curtal
   C. saltarello
   D. pavane
   E. basse danse

7. A gaillarde was frequently paired with a(n) _____.

   A. lute
   B. bassadanse
   C. pavane
   D. consort
   E. toccata

8. A Renaissance courtier would be unlikely to have danced to a(n) _____.

   A. basse danse
   B. passamezzo
   C. pavane
   D. lute
   E. intonazione

9. Renaissance composers wrote many songs for solo voice and _____.

   A. recorder
   B. jack
   C. canzona

    D. lute
    E. tiento

10. A toccata was an instrumental piece in _____ style.

    A. dance
    B. chanson
    C. improvisatory
    D. woodwind
    E. consort

True-False/Justification

1. Because words were so important to Renaissance music, instrumental music declined after the close of the Middle Ages.

2. The vihuela was a Spanish plucked chordophone.

3. The Renaissance cornett made a brilliant sound resembling that of the modern trumpet.

4. A broken consort combined haut and bas instruments.

5. The organ was the only keyboard instrument known to Renaissance musicians.

6. Only lute players used tablature.

7. Instruments were commonly used together with voices in the sixteenth century.

8. The passamezzo and pavane most commonly used duple rhythm.

9. Renaissance composers did not have means to unify extended instrumental works.

10. Improvisational pieces were often paired with other instrumental or vocal pieces in the Renaissance.

Short Essay

Compare the characteristic instrumental ensemble of the Renaissance with that of the Middle Ages, and explain how scoring relates to texture in each period.

Discuss at least two different relationships between vocal and instrumental music in the Renaissance.

ANSWERS TO SAMPLE TEST QUESTIONS

Multiple Choice

1. D   consort
2. B   crumhorn
3. E   keyboard
4. D   viola da gamba
5. A   ricercar
6. C   saltarello
7. C   pavane
8. E   intonazione
9. D   lute
10. C   improvisatory

True-False/Justification

1. F   Instrumental music continued to expand during the Renaissance.

2. T   The vihuela is an ancestor of the modern guitar.

3. F   The cornet's sound was quite restrained and matched well with choral voices.

4. F   A broken consort employed different types of instruments but only within the haut or, more commonly, bas classification.

5. F   Renaissance musicians knew the clavichord, harpsichord, and virginal.

6. F   Keyboardists had a version of tablature for their instruments.

7. T   Instrumentalists could double or substitute for voice parts in polyphonic vocal music.

8. T   Passamezzo and pavane contrasted with the saltarello and gaillarde, which had triple or compound rhythm.

9. F   The variation principle allowed for extended treatments of melodies or harmonic structures, and it also linked contrasting pieces in dance pairs.

10. T   The terms intonazione, prelude, and preambulum all designate an improvisational piece that served to introduce something else.

CHAPTER 10

THE REFORMATION

CHAPTER OVERVIEW

The various branches of the Reformation arose from the problems within the church and from outside developments. The particular concerns and attitudes of different reformers led to corresponding developments in sacred music.

Martin Luther supported music as an important element in religious experience. He revised the Mass, and Lutheranism cultivated the chorale for the everyday singing of the German Christians. A large body of chorales was created, and these served as an important stimulus for German polyphonic compositions.

Unlike Luther, Jean Calvin took a very conservative view of music in the church. The musical repertoire of Calvinism consisted of the psalter, which became the forerunners of modern hymnbooks.

The English Reformation produced a wealth of elaborate music in the form of Services derived from the Roman liturgy and anthems. Anthems included both motet-like full anthems and verse anthems, which employed soloists, instruments, and choir.

The Roman church responded to the Reformation in the Counter-Reformation, guided by the Council of Trent. The liturgy was simplified, and guidelines for musical style were espoused in order to assure the music's appropriateness and the clarity of the words. Palestrina's music represents the conservative ideal of the Counter-Reformation aesthetic; some of his prominent contemporaries explored more progressive styles.

OBJECTIVES

1. To help the student understand the reasons for the different reformation movements and their effects on music aesthetics.

2. To acquaint the student with the different major genres of Reformation music—chorale, psalter, Service, and anthem—and their styles.

3. To give the student an understanding of the aesthetics and style of music in the Counter-Reformation.

TERMS, NAMES, AND CONCEPTS

Reformation
Martin Luther
Deutsche Messe
chorale
Johann Walter
cantional style
chorale motet
Jean Calvin
Louis Bourgeois
psalter
Henry VIII
Great Service
Short Service
anthem
> full anthem
> verse anthem
Counter-Reformation
Council of Trent
Palestrina
Jesuits
Tomas Luis da Victoria
Roland de Lassus
William Byrd

CLASSROOM APPROACHES, ASSIGNMENTS, TOPICS FOR DISCUSSION

Musical Aesthetics of the Reformers

Students should research the ideas of Luther and Calvin about music and compare them to earlier conceptions of music in society and religion. Luther believed that music was an important component of the education of young people, echoing the philosophies of Plato and Aristotle. Luther's and Calvin's contrasting attitudes toward music in religion recapitulate the dichotomy that St. Augustine faced.

Remind students that they have already considered the relation of musical style to the proper roles of sacred music. Students should discuss how the church dealt with this problem in the sixteeenth century. Which church leaders took a conservative view, and what stylistic traits marked the music that resulted? Which leaders took a more liberal view, and what sort of music resulted? Discuss again the students' own opinions about the pros and cons of theologians determining appropriate musical styles for church music. Have any students' positions changed since the earlier discussion of this topic?

Liturgy and Musical Practice in Protestant Traditions

Encourage students to attend a service in a Lutheran and/or a
Calvinist (Presbyterian, Reformed, etc.) church. They should report in
class what elements of worship the regular services in these church
share with the Mass and which items are characteristic of the
Protestant traditions. They should also report on the music itself,
noting whether chorales or psalms are sung. If the choir sings an
anthem, the students should note both its place in the liturgy and its
musical style.

Students should become familiar with the most famous melodies of
Lutheranism and Calvinism, "Ein' feste Burg" and Old Hundredth.
Have the students sing those tunes in class. Discuss their melodic
contours, rhythmic character, and harmonic implications. *Students
sometimes acquire from a colloquialism used in music theory classes the
misunderstanding that a chorale was a four-part harmony exercise—be sure
they are disabused of this idea!* If students are prepared to do so, assign
them to make a harmonic analysis of J.S. Bach's settings of each
melody.

MUSIC FOR STUDY

Martin Luther (1483–1546), "Aus tiefer Not"
Johann Walter (1496–1570), "Aus tiefer Not"
Arnold von Bruck (ca. 1500–1554), "Aus tiefer Not"

Style features

Luther's original chorale represents the style of this repertoire.
The form of the stanza, aab, resembles that of the contemporary
Meistersingers' songs. Word painting occurs on the melody's second
note, but applies only to the first stanza.

Walter's arrangement sets the chorale with the melody in the
tenor, a characteristic trait of German Renaissance music. The first
sections are generally in homorhythmic style; the last section
becomes more contrapuntally animated.

The setting of the chorale by Arnold von Bruck shows the
technique of the chorale motet.

The harmonization by Bach provided here (1724) offers an
example of his approach. The setting is in cantional style, with the
chorale in the soprano part. Particularly important are the
Baroque affective interpretation of the textual content and Bach's
solution to the problem of creating effective cadences for a modal
melody within a more modern harmonic syntax.

Score

EMH, 213–217

Louis Bourgeois (ca. 1510–1561)

Style features

The example is a four-part polyphonic setting of a psalm in homorhythmic style. The melody is the tenor voice. The rhythmic structure follows the natural declamation of French, flowing to the stressed final syllables of the phrases.

Score

HAM 1, 144

Orlando Gibbons (1583–1625), "This is the record of John"

Style features

This example illustrates the style of the verse anthem, set for countertenor soloist, viols (or organ), and choir.

Scores

HAM 1, 195–198

SSHS 1, 112–116

Recordings

Orlando Gibbons, *Anthems and Songs of Praise*, 2. The Clerkes of Oxenford; David Wullstan, dir. Nonesuch H71391.

Orlando Gibbons, *Anthems, Madrigals, and Fantasias.* Deller Consort; Schola Cantorum Basiliensis. Archiv ARC 3053.

Tudor Church Music. Choir of King's College Chapel, Cambridge; Hugh McLean, Simon Preston, organ; Jacobean Consort of Viols; Boris Ord, David Willcocks, dir. Argo ZRG 5151.

Tudor Church Music. Choir of King's College, Cambridge; John Butt, organ; Philip Ledger, dir. Musical Heritage Society MHS 7039.

Palestrina (ca. 1525–1594), "Veni sponsa Christi" and Missa Veni sponsa Christi, *Kyrie*

Style features

Palestrina's motet derives its points of imitation by paraphrasing the successive phrases of the chant antiphon "Veni sponsa Christi." The Mass based on the motet is a good example of the parody technique.

Scores

AMSS, 51–57—chant on p. 5

 * EMH, 224–232—chant on p. 227

(*MM, 86–90 presents the first Agnus Dei from the Mass and the chant, but it does not include the motet. The music is transposed down a major second in this score.)

Roland de Lassus (ca. 1532–1594), "Tristis est anima mea"

Style features

Lassus's approach to the motet, as shown in this work, contrasts to Palestrina's by its vivid use of wordpainting (at "vos fugam capietis" the composer not only employs fuga but also remembers that the disciples fled downhill from the Mount of Olives) and mood evocation ("mortem" sounds especially bleak because the cadential harmony is an open fifth).

Scores

EMH, 233–236

 * MM, 78–85

SAMPLE TEST QUESTIONS

Multiple Choice

1. A(n) _____ is a German Lutheran hymn tune and its text.

    A. anthem
    B. Deutsche Messe
    C. chorale
    D. cantional
    E. psalter

2. The composer _____ gave important support to Martin Luther's efforts to create a German Protestant musical repertoire.

    A. Ulrich Zwingli
    B. Johann Walter
    C. Heinrich Isaac
    D. Feste Burg
    E. Roland de Lassus

3. Many of the early chorales were _____ of Roman Catholic chant or popular songs.

    A. polyphonic settings
    B. motets
    C. Services
    D. parodies
    E. psalters

4. When a hymn tune is set in familiar style with the melody in the topmost voice, the setting is said to be in _____ style.

    A. cantional
    B. Lutheran
    C. Palestrina
    D. anthem
    E. chorale motet

5. The composer Louis Bourgeois served the branch of the Reformation led by _____.

    A. Henry VIII
    B. Ulrich Zwingli
    C. the Council of Trent
    D. Jean Calvin
    E. Martin Luther

6. For the Huguenots, the _____ formed the only legitimate source for the texts of sacred music.

    A. Council of Trent
    B. Mass Ordinary
    C. chorales
    D. Great Service
    E. book of Psalms

7. The break between the English and the Roman Catholic church was made by _____.

    A. John Calvin
    B. Sternhold and Hopkins
    C. Henry VIII
    D. Queen Mary
    E. William Byrd

8. The English equivalent of the Latin motet is the _____ .

    A. antiphon
    B. anthem
    C. Great Service

  D. chorale motet
  E. Gradualia

9. The_____ established general principles for Roman
   Catholic music after the middle of the sixteenth century.

   A. Pope
   B. Huguenots
   C. Council of Trent
   D. Jesuits
   E. Magnum opus musicum

10. _____ became the model composer for the music of the
    Counter-Reformation because of the clarity and conservative
    character of his music.

    A. Johann Walter
    B. Jean Calvin
    C. Roland de Lassus
    D. William Byrd
    E. Palestrina

True-False/Justification

1. Martin Luther was not musically inclined and was always deeply
   concerned that music be strictly limited in the church.

2. The style of the Latin motet was adapted to German words and
   melodic material for the Lutheran church.

3. Jean Calvin encouraged the formation of large church choirs of lay
   men and women to sing polyphonic anthems and lead the service
   music in local parish churches.

4. The Calvinist psalters influenced music in branches of the
   Reformation other than Calvinism.

5. The Reformation in England was precipitated partly by political
   factors.

6. A verse anthem is a strophic hymn with at least three stanzas, all
   sung a cappella by a choir of men and boys.

7. Pope Paul III convened the Council of Trent primarily to review the
   musical practices and styles of the church.

8. All Roman Catholic choral music after the Council of Trent
   maintained a placid and restrained character.

9. Roland de Lassus, unlike other Franco-Netherlands composers of the Renaissance, did not leave his homeland but remained there as the leading Calvinist composer.

10. The texts of sacred music were very important to thinkers about music and religion in the sixteenth century.

Short Essay

Briefly explain how the leaders of change in the different branches of the church in the sixteenth century influenced developments in the style of sacred music.

Describe at least two genres of Reformation church music that relied on the style of Roman Catholic sacred music in the sixteenth century.

ANSWERS TO SAMPLE TEST QUESTIONS

Multiple Choice

1. C   chorale
2. B   Johann Walter
3. D   parodies
4. A   cantional
5. D   Jean Calvin
6. E   book of Psalms
7. C   Henry VIII
8. B   anthem
9. C   Council of Trent
10. E   Palestrina

True-False/Justification

1. F   Luther was a music lover and amateur player, and he vigorously promoted church music, even composing some himself.

2. T   The chorale motet consisted of a setting of each phrase of a chorale in turn, using the techniques employed in a Latin motet.

3. F   Calvin allowed only congregational singing of monophonic psalms.

4. T   Some French psalms were adapted as Lutheran chorales, and many denominations' later hymnbooks were based on the psalters.

5. T   Henry VIII separated the English church from the Roman church because he rejected the church's authority to uphold or annul his marriages.

6. F   A verse anthem exploits the contrast of solo singer(s), instruments, and choir.

7. F   The Council of Trent considered many matters of theology and practice, of which music was only one.

8. F   The music of Tomas Luis da Victoria represents the more impassioned and emotional type of Catholic music.

9. F   Lassus traveled to Italy and Germany and was a Catholic composer.

10. T   The Reformers sought music in the vernacular so that common people could understand worship, and the Counter-Reformation stressed clarity of the words in polyphonic settings.

CHAPTER 11

THE WANING OF THE RENAISSANCE

CHAPTER OVERVIEW

As the close of the sixteenth century approached, the Renaissance musical style became more sophisticated and increasingly varied. In Italy the techniques of madrigal composition reached a peak, sometimes placing considerable demands on the skills of the singers. There developed several subgenres of the madrigal, as well as several related lighter genres of Italian secular polyphonic song. A manneristic approach also appeared, notably in the madrigals of Carlo Gesualdo.

The Italian style came into vogue in England beginning in 1588. English composers drew on the brilliant flowering of Tudor poetry and created an outstanding repertoire of vocal ensemble music. In France composers concentrated on matters of declamation and a simpler style in the vaudeville and air de cour.

A special development associated primarily with Venice was the cultivation of polychoral music. Although its greatest proponents were composers working at the basilica of St. Mark's in Venice, the style was extended from sacred vocal music to instrumental works and to the madrigal.

OBJECTIVES

1. To help the student understand the stylistic developments in the music of the late Renaissance.

2. To introduce the student to the various genres of secular vocal music in late Renaissance Italy, England, and France.

3. To familiarize the student with the Venetian polychoral technique.

TERMS, NAMES, AND CONCEPTS

Luca Marenzio
Torquato Tasso
intermedio
pastoral plays

Battista Guarini
divisions
Lucrezia Bendidio, Laura Peverara, Tarquinia Molza
Luzzasco Luzzaschi
canzonetta
balletta
villanella
Carlo Gesualdo
Musica transalpina
Nicholas Yonge
canzonet
ballett
The Triumphs of Oriana
simultaneous cross-relation
Jean-Antoine Baïf
Claude LeJeune
musique mesurée
vaudeville
air de cour
cori spezzati
Andrea Gabrieli
Giovanni Gabrieli

CLASSROOM APPROACHES, ASSIGNMENTS, TOPICS FOR DISCUSSION

Approaches to Text Setting

Give students one or more examples of late Renaissance Italian or English madrigal poetry and ask them to discuss the ways in which a composer might have created music to suit the words. Then listen in class to a setting of each text. Discuss what qualities in a text would make it especially appealing to madrigal composers in this period.

Draw students' attention to the developments in rhythm in France in the sixteenth century compared to those of five centuries earlier. Compare the ideas of the generation of Leonin to those of Baif. Students should recognize that the developments in both periods relate to an academic approach to the relationship between poetic rhythm and music.

St. Mark's and the Polychoral Style

Assign students to research the actual placement of the performers in St. Mark's basilica in Venice and to mark their possible locations on a plan of the church. (The use of entirely separate galleries has been called into question. See James H. Moore, "The *Vespero delli Cinque Laudate* and the Role of *Salmi Spezzati* at St. Mark's," *Journal of the American Musicological Society* 34 [1981], 277.)

MUSIC FOR STUDY

Luca Marenzio (1553–1599), "Solo e pensoso"

Style features

In treating the text, a Petrarch sonnet, Marenzio found musical ideas from the many images the poetry provided. The madrigal's structure reflects the division of the sonnet into octave and sestet.

Score

* NAWM 1, 276–287

Maddalena Casulana, "Morte. Che voi? Te chiamo."

Style features

The scoring is especially high for the tenor and bass parts. The text is a dialogue between the poet and death; both interlocutors' lines are shared among the four vocal parts. The words "Si fa!" produce a setting that focuses on the notes associated with those syllables in solzmization.

Score

HAMW, 18–21

Carlo Gesualdo (ca. 1560–1613), "Mercè grido piangendo"

Style features

Besides using word-painting to mirror poetic imagery, Gesualdo pressed the harmonic language of his time to maneristic extremes in the service of emotionalism. Noteworthy are the characteristic cross-relations. The phrases also break off abruptly, as if to suggest a speaker unable to continue because of emotion.

Score

SSMS, 138–141

Recording

Carlo Gesualdo, *Madrigaux*. Les Arts Florissants; William Christie, dir. Harmonia mundi 901268 (CD).

Claude LeJeune (1528–1600), "Revecy venir le printemps"

Style features

The hemiola rhythm is determined by the principles of *musique mesurée*. The structure of the work is a series of verses in various scorings alternating with a five-part refrain.

Score

* NAWM 1, 243–258

Thomas Weelkes (ca. 1575–1623), "O Care, Thou Wilt Despatch Me"

Style features

This madrigal ironically employs the fa-las of the ballett to suggest the cheering effect of music, but the music itself indicates that the poet remains uncheered. The harmony shows the influence of the late Renaissance Italian style; a striking simultaneous cross-relation appears in measure 39.

Score

* NAWM 1, 293–301

Giovanni Gabrieli (ca. 1553–1612), "In ecclesiis"

Style features

Three choirs are called for, one of solo voices, one of choral voices, and one of instruments (three cornetti, viola, and two sackbuts), as well as organ. The clearly soloistic writing for solo singers contrasts with the simple homorhythmic style used in the ritornello sections, which feature exchanges between choirs.

Scores

* EMH, 313–325

  HAM 1, 175–179

Giovanni Gabrieli, "Sonata pian e forte"

Style features

The two ensembles in this canzona are distinguished by the use of cornetto as the soprano voice in one and violino in the other; the remaining parts in each group are for sackbuts. The dynamic contrasts match the distinctions between passages for the separate ensembles (piano) and those for the combined forces (forte).

Score

HAM 1, 198–200

SAMPLE TEST QUESTIONS

Multiple Choice

1. The most sophisticated genre of secular music in late Renaissance Italy was the _____.

   A. balletto
   B. villanella
   C. madrigal
   D. vaudeville
   E. intermedio

2. Embellishments added to performers' parts in music of the Renaissance were sometimes called _____.

   A. intermedi
   B. divisions
   C. canzonette
   D. cori spezzati
   E. Musica transalpina

3. The most harmonically adventurous composer of late Renaissance Italian was the mannerist _____.

   A. Battista Guarini
   B. Luzzasco Luzzaschi
   C. Claude LeJeune
   D. Giovanni Gabrieli
   E. Carlo Gesualdo

4. In _____ the English became aware of the latest Italian style of composition through a publication of translated Italian madrigals by Nicholas Yonge.

   A. 1554
   B. 1563
   C. 1575
   D. 1588
   E. 1594

5. A particular expressive mannerism in English polyphony around 1600 was the _____.

   A. simultaneous cross-relation
   B. mannerism

C. *Triumphs of Oriana*
D. *Musica transalpina*
E. ballett

6. Poets and composers in _____ in the late sixteenth century explored a type of poetic declamation that rather strictly interpreted the syllables of a text as short and long values.

A. England
B. France
C. Germany
D. Italy
E. Spain

7. The _____ was a type of dance song that used the nonsense syllables "fa la" in its refrain.

A. air de cour
B. balletto
C. canzonetta
D. divisions
E. vaudeville

8. The development of scoring for separate choirs of voices and/or instruments is most closely associated with composers who worked in _____.

A. England
B. Ferrara
C. Paris
D. Rome
E. Venice

9. The composer Giovanni Gabrieli worked as _____ at the famous basilica of St. Mark's.

A. maestro di cappella
B. singer
C. organist
D. priest
E. music theorist

10. The polychoral style is sometimes called _____.

A. airs de cour
B. balletto
C. cori spezzati
D. divisions
E. mannerism

True-False/Justification

1. Because he was employed by the church in Rome Palestrina composed only sacred music.

2. The works of Luca Marenzio represent a peak in the technique of using poetry to inspire musical ideas.

3. Dramatic literature provided important sources of texts for late Renaissance madrigal composers.

4. One of the significant trends in late Renaissance music was the rise of virtuosity among singers.

5. Unlike the end of the Middle Ages, the late Renaissance did not produce a mannerist phase.

6. *The Triumphs of Oriana* was a musical drama that recounted the success of English colonization in the orient.

7. An academic approach was characteristic of aesthetic thinking in France.

8. The vaudeville began in France as a variety entertainment with comic acts and burlesque songs and dances.

9. The polychoral style was invented by Giovanni Gabrieli at St. Mark's cathedral.

10. By the end of the sixteenth century the cosmopolitan style of Renaissance music had given way to a variety of styles associated with different genres and places.

Short Essay

Summarize the development of the Italian madrigal from the beginning to the end of the sixteenth century, citing some of the most important madrigal composers whose works exemplify different stages in its history.

Choose at least three different musical genres from the late sixteenth century to illustrate the contrasts in musical style that existed at the end of the Renaissance.

ANSWERS TO SAMPLE TEST QUESTIONS

Multiple Choice

1. C   madrigal
2. B   divisions

3. E   Carlo Gesualdo
4. D   1588
5. A   simultaneous cross-relation
6. B   France
7. B   balletto
8. E   Venice
9. C   organist
10. C   cori spezzati

True-False/Justification

1. F   Palestrina composed madrigals, though these are
         characteristically restrained in style.

2. T   In Marenzio's madrigals almost every musical detail can be
         traced to the text.

3. T   Many madrigal texts came from the pastoral plays staged at
         Italian courts and from the intermedi.

4. T   The great women singers of Ferrara demonstrated this
         virtuosity and inspired remarkable compositions.

5. F   Mannerism can be found in late Renaissance painting,
         literature, and music.

6. F   *The Triumphs of Oriana* was a collection of madrigals in honor of
         Queen Elizabeth.

7. T   Baïf's Academy of Poetry and Music and the vers mesuree are
         examples of the French academic inclination.

8. F   The vaudeville was a simple, strophic song in sixteenth-
         century France.

9. F   Polychoral scoring was not a new invention in the late sixteenth
         century and was not limited to St. Mark's.

10. T   Popular and serious styles differed in the late sixteenth
         century, and different countries developed contrasting styles.

CHAPTER 12

THE ARRIVAL OF THE BAROQUE

CHAPTER OVERVIEW

The period in the history of art and music that we call Baroque
corresponds to the period of Rationalism in the history of thought. The
term *baroque* suggests that the style of art was excessively ornamented
or distorted, and this was a characteristic of a great deal of art during
the period. More important, however, were the doctrine of the
affections as the aesthetic basis of the arts and the intention of the
artists to move the observer's or audience's passions.

The aesthetic background for Baroque music was articulated by the
Florentine camerata in the late sixteenth century. Vincenzo Galilei
proposed that the model for musical expression should be rhetoric.

The rhetorical model and the desire to imitate the music of the
ancient Greeks led to the development of a new texture, monody or
homophony. In this period homophonic texture consisted of a solo
melodic line and basso continuo accompaniment.

Also important in the creation of a Baroque musical style was a
change in the ideal of scoring. The Renaissance ideal of a homogeneous
sound gave way to the exploitation of timbral contrast. The new scoring,
called concertato, employed different sound forces to set off contrasting
musical functions within a piece.

The third decisive stylistic determinant of Baroque music was a
new attitude toward harmony. Unprepared and unresolved treatments
of dissonance, which Claudio Monteverdi called "seconda prattica,"
found a rhetorical justification because they created more powerful
affections in the listener.

OBJECTIVES

1. To help the student understand the philosophical background and
   aesthetic foundations of Baroque music.

2. To introduce the student to the principles of basso continuo
   homophony.

3. To give the student an understanding of the principle of concertato
   scoring.

4. To help the student understand the rationale and style of Baroque harmony.

TERMS, NAMES, AND CONCEPTS

Rationalism
baroque
affections, passions
Florentine camerata
Giovanni de' Bardi
Vincenzo Galilei
Girolamo Mei
monody
homophonic texture
aria
Giulio Caccini
Le nuove musiche
passaggi
accento
esclamatione
trillo
gruppo
basso seguente
basso continuo, thoroughbass
figured bass
concertato
G. M. Artusi
Claudio Monteverdi
Giulio Cesare Monteverdi
prima prattica, stile antico
seconda prattica, stile moderno

CLASSROOM APPROACHES, ASSIGNMENTS, TOPICS FOR DISCUSSION

Baroque Aesthetics

Have students define ethos, affection, and emotion in such a way that they clearly differentiate among these ideas. They should observe that ethos applies to human character or personality, while affection refers to moods or states of mind. Affection is more simple and static than emotion, which we think of as complex and fluctuating.

Read with the class Milton's "L'Allegro" and "Il Penseroso." Discuss the contrast between the affections of joy and melancholy. Do both have value for the poet? What dominant images can students identify that Milton used to convey each of these affections?

Listen in class to the masque of the affections (beginning with the recitative No. 45, "Sweep the string") in the third part of Handel's *Solomon*. Have the class list the different affections and identify the poetic images and the musical style elements Handel used to convey each affection.

Assign students to write a critique of one of the Italian or English Renaissance madrigals they studied earlier, modeled on Vincenzo Galilei's criticism of the style in the *Dialogo della musica antica e della moderna*. They should look for both characteristics Galilei would approve and those he would attack.

Musical Style

Assign students to write out an ornamented version of a simple vocal part from an early seventeenth-century monodic song, using the ornaments Caccini specifies in *Le nuove musiche*. Have students perform their work in class. They should be able to discuss the musical or textual effects of their ornaments.

Have students realize the figured bass of a song from Caccini's *Le nuove musiche*. They should attempt to do so at sight at the keyboard (guitar players may wish to attempt this on their instrument), then write out a realization in keyboard score. Students who have not studied much music theory may only be able to strive for accuracy; more advanced students may be asked to produce some rhythmic animation and interest in their work. Discuss the problems that playing from a figured (or unfigured) bass poses for the performer. How thorough and helpful do the students find Caccini's figures? Discuss how different players might produce very different realizations of the same figured bass. What factors might influence a keyboard player's style of basso continuo playing? Could one accurate performance be less appropriate than another for a particular piece? Why or why not?

In class analyze a seconda prattica piece by Monteverdi (e.g., the madrigal "Cruda Amarilli" or a later madrigal for two voices and continuo), identifying each type of dissonance and whether it is permissible or impermissible within the rules of sixteenth-century counterpoint (i.e., unaccented passing tones or suspensions). Have the students try to show how passages would appear without the dissonances. A helpful model for this may be found in Christoph Bernhard's paired musical examples explaining dissonance figures; see "The Treatises of Christoph Bernhard," trans. Walter Hilse, in *The Music Forum* 3, ed. William J. Mitchell and Felix Salzer (New York: Columbia University Press, 1973), pp. 77–120. Students should discuss the textual/affective justification for the use of dissonance.

MUSIC FOR STUDY

Giulio Caccini (ca. 1550–1618), "Perfidissimo volto"

Style features

This song, on a text by Guarini, is a madrigal in monodic texture with figured bass from *Le nuove musiche*. The melodic style is rhythmically flexible, and ornamentation in addition to that written out by Caccini is possible. The piece uses concertato scoring in the sense that the contrasting timbres of voice and continuo serve contrasting musical functions.

Scores

> * EMH, 287–291

> * NAWM 1, 315–318

Claudio Monteverdi (1567–1643), "Cruda Amarilli"

Style features

> "Cruda Amarilli" is the classic example of seconda prattica harmony, since it was singled out by Artusi to illustrate his objections to the modern style. The text justifies the striking harmonic idiom.

Scores

> * EMH, 278–282

> * NAWM 1, 319–323

> SSHS 1, 157–161

SAMPLE TEST QUESTIONS

Multiple Choice

1. The philosophical movement that corresponds to the time of the Baroque in music was _____.

    A. absolutism
    B. humor
    C. humanism
    D. rationalism
    E. enlightenment

2. The word _____ generally means overly ornamented, distorted, bizarre, or eccentric.

    A. affection
    B. baroque
    C. concertato
    D. stile antico
    E. humor

3. A_____ is a mood or state of mind; the six basic ones were
    love, hate, joy, sorrow, wonder, and desire.

    A. stile antico
    B. baroque
    C. camerata
    D. passion
    E. seconda prattica

4. New aesthetic principles for music were articulated in the late
    sixteenth century by a group of intellectuals who met in the city of
    _____.

    A. Paris
    B. Rome
    C. Berlin
    D. Venice
    E. Florence

5. Vincenzo Galilei recommended that, in order to understand how
    musical expression should function, composers ought to attend
    _____.

    A. meetings in the house of Giovanni de' Bardi
    B. church
    C. the university
    D. the theater
    E. concerts

6. The musical texture of solo voice with accompaniment by a lute or
    keyboard instrument is called _____.

    A. seconda prattica
    B. baroque
    C. monody
    D. esclamatione
    E. basso continuo

7. An Italian strophic song in the early seventeenth century was
    identified as a(n) _____.

    A. accento
    B. aria
    C. madrigal
    D. concertato
    E. basso seguente

8. For his collection of songs published in 1602 as *Le nuove musiche,*
    _____ wrote a preface that explained vocal
    ornamentation and the use of figured bass.

    A. René Descartes
    B. Giovanni de' Bardi
    C. Giulio Caccini
    D. Vincenzo Galilei
    E. Claudio Monteverdi

9. Since the beginning of the seventeenth century, the term
    _____ has implied any use of contrasting voices and/or
    instruments with separate functions.

    A. stile antico
    B. camerata
    C. concertato
    D. basso continuo
    E. baroque

10. The concept of second prattica has to do with the musical style
    element_____.

    A. scoring
    B. dynamics
    C. melody
    D. rhythm
    E. harmony

True-False/Justification

1. Baroque art is based on the promotion of irrational emotionalism.

2. Elaborate ornamentation characterizes all Baroque art, literature,
    and music.

3. *The Passions of the Soul* was a series of madrigals composed by
    Vincenzo Galilei to illustrate the proper approach to musical
    expression.

4. Giovanni de' Bardi was most important to music as a patron of the
    arts and intellectual discourse.

5. Vincenzo Galilei rejected both the formal rules of sixteenth-century
    counterpoint and the Renaissance madrigalists' methods of
    interpreting texts in their music.

6. In the early seventeenth century composers developed monody,
    which consisted of a text set monophonically for a single voice .

7. An early seventeenth-century aria was an elaborate piece for a virtuoso singer with orchestral accompaniment.

8. An early Baroque madrigal for solo singer resembled a polyphonic Renaissance madrigal in its approach to musical form.

9. Concertato scoring always required at least two different types of instruments or voice(s) and instrument(s).

10. Claudio Monteverdi coined the term "seconda prattica" to explain the difference between an earlier style of melodic writing and the modern style.

Short Essay

Explain how the doctrine of the affections related to music in both theory and practice in the Baroque period.

Contrast the musical styles of the Renaissance and the Baroque with regard to scoring, melody, harmony, and texture.

ANSWERS TO SAMPLE TEST QUESTIONS

Multiple Choice

1. D   rationalism
2. B   baroque
3. D   passion
4. E   Florence
5. D   the theater
6. C   monody
7. B   aria
8. C   Giulio Caccini
9. C   concertato
10. E harmony

True-False/Justification

1. F   The art of the Baroque derives from the rationalist understanding of human feelings as affections or passions.

2. F   Much of the painting, writing, and music of the Baroque is quite simple.

3. F   *The Passions of the Soul* was a treatise by the French philosopher René Descartes.

4. T   He hosted the discussions of the Florentine camerata in the 1570s.

5. T   Galilei felt the rules of harmony were artificial and that the poetic method of text-setting failed to capture the affections of poetry.

6. F   Monody in the seventeenth century included an accompaniment and thus meant a homophonic texture.

7. F   The term *aria* in the early Baroque period designated a simple strophic song.

8. T   Both sixteenth- and seventeenth-century madrigals used free rather than strophic form.

9. T   Timbre contrast is an essential component of concertato style.

10. F   "Seconda prattica" referred to the new style of harmony.

CHAPTER 13

THE EARLY BAROQUE

CHAPTER OVERVIEW

The invention of opera took place around 1600, led by the Florentine camerata. The early operas took their subjects from Greek mythology. They employed monody in order to present individual characters on the stage and created the recitative style to make the vocal lines more speechlike. The first masterpiece in the new genre was Monteverdi's *Orfeo*, written in Mantua in 1607. Opera soon spread to other Italian cities, notably Rome and Venice, where the first public opera theater opened in 1637. By mid-century there were clearly differentiated singing styles used for different affective/dramatic purposes—recitative, bel canto, and florid aria style.

Vocal chamber music with one or more singers accompanied by basso continuo became widespread in the early seventeenth century. Trio texture—two voices and continuo—was especially effective. In addition to the free-form madrigal and simple strophic aria a popular form was strophic variation, often over a standard bass formula. The term *cantata* was first used for songs in strophic or strophic variation form; it later came to designate multisectional vocal pieces.

Composers continued to employ the stile antico and a cappella scoring for sacred music, and the concertato style also became prominent, creating the sacred concerto. The modern style with free use of dissonance figures soon appeared in church music as well. The incorporation of dramatic means into religious musical practice produced the oratorio in the middle part of the seventeenth century.

A variety of developments in instrumental music took place in these years. The ricercar was superseded by the polyphonic fantasia on a single subject, while the canzona evolved into the multisectional sonata with basso continuo. Variation forms continued in popularity with partitas and, in Lutheran Germany, the chorale partita for church organists. The dance pairs of the Renaissance expanded into the suite. Improvisatory-style compositions also thrived.

OBJECTIVES

1. To help the student understand the origin and early developments in opera.

2. To introduce the student to the genres, textures, and forms of early Baroque vocal chamber music.

3. To acquaint the student with the styles of the sacred concerto and oratorio.

4. To give the student an understanding of the development of Baroque instrumental music out of that of the Renaissance.

TERMS, NAMES, AND CONCEPTS

Marco Scacchi
stylus ecclesiasticus, stylus cubicularis, stylus theatralis
madrigal dialogues
madrigal comedies
opera
Ottavio Rinuccini
Jacopo Peri
stile rappresentativo
recitative
Emilio de' Cavalieri
Alessandro Striggio
ritornello
Stefano Landi
Francesco Cavalli
Antonio Cesti
bel canto
florid style
stile concitato
trio texture
strophic variation
    romanesca
    ruggiero
    chaconne
    passacaglia
lamento bass
cantata
stylus gravis
sacred concerto
Lodovico Grossi da Viadana
Heinrich Schütz
oratorio
historia
oratorio latino, oratoria volgare
testo, historicus
Giacomo Carissimi
Michael Praetorius
monothematic fantasia
    subject
    exposition

sonata
trio sonata
partita
chorale partita
Samuel Scheidt
suite
    prelude
    allemande
    courante
    sarabande
    gigue
Johann Jacob Froberger
Johann Hermann Schein

CLASSROOM APPROACHES, ASSIGNMENTS, TOPICS FOR DISCUSSION

Opera

Have students research the halls and theaters in which early operas were performed, the costumes, the stage designs and special effects. If possible, show in class a film of a reproduction of one of Monteverdi's operas. Were the sets and costumes intended to represent accurately those of ancient Greece and Rome? What were the possibilities and limitations of stagecraft? Discuss what assumptions early-seventeenth-century audiences of the time made about realism and stylization. What were the purposes of the opera? To what extent does a modern audience's appreciation of the text, music, and staging of these operas depend on understanding their historical situation?

In class, construct a two-column diagram showing the dramatic and musical structure of Monteverdi's *Orfeo*. In one column students should identify the location and basic action of each act, listing under those headings the major events of the act and marking its dramatic climax. In the second column they should locate the main musical numbers, placing them opposite the corresponding moments in the column showing the action. They should determine which musical pieces provide entertaining interludes, which establish the dramatic situations, and which further the action. Discuss the affections conveyed by some of the major numbers.

Vocal and Instrumental Chamber Music

Students should be able to find short vocal chamber works and instrumental pieces from the early Baroque that they can perform competently in class; modern instruments may certainly be used. Follow performances with discussion of the differences between period instruments and modern ones, including the advantages and disadvantages of each and the value to the modern instrumentalist of understanding the period instruments' sound. Discuss the unnotated aspects of the music—ornamentation, continuo realization, and expression. Students should be able to state what affection they thought the music intended to convey.

Assign students to compose a piece in strophic variation form on the romanesca or ruggiero. Vocalists may wish to set a strophic poem as a song or duet (John Donne's "Song: Go, and catch a falling star" or "Song: Sweetest love, I do not go" might serve). Instrumentalists should compose for their own instruments. An interesting possibility is to have jazz players make a jazz arrangement on these early Baroque harmonic frameworks. Students should perform and discuss their compositions in class.

Sacred music

Have students research the liturgical practice of a Mass in Rome in the seventeenth century and then compile scores for the various movements of Ordinary and Proper to make up a complete Mass. Discuss the effect of the combination of various musical styles in the service.

Assign singers to compose a brief passage of biblical text in the style of a sacred concerto for solo voice and basso continuo by Viadana, Monteverdi, or Schutz. They should determine the appropriate affection and employ dissonance and melodic style accordingly. Students should perform and discuss their work in class.

In class outline in table or chart form similarities and differences between opera and oratorio in terms of text structure, musical forces and styles used, and staging.

MUSIC FOR STUDY

Claudio Monteverdi, Orfeo

Style features

(The opera represents all the principles and techniques of the genre in its time. Only a few passages of particular interest can be pointed out here.)

Toccata—The "toccata" serves as overture. It is harmonically limited, but a good representation of fanfare style in the early Baroque. (This piece was also later incorporated into Monteverdi's Vespers of 1610.)

Prologue—Such an opening was traditional in the early opera as in the dramatic models of the time. It is a set of strophic variations separated by ritornelli.

Score

* NAWM 1, 354–359

Act II—The scene beginning with Orfeo's strophic aria (with ritornelli) "Vi ricorda o boschi ombrosi" illustrates a set number. It offers a very clear example of hemiola. The scene in which the Messenger delivers the news of Euridice's death demonstrates recitative style. Orfeo's famous lament "Tu se' morta" shows how Monteverdi synthesized the mimetic treatment of words as in the Renaissance with the use of affective dissonance. The scene concludes with a chorus that both establishes the affective spirit and articulates the dramatic action.

Scores

* EMH, 355–363

* NAWM 1, 360–361

* MM, 124–128

Act III—"Possente spirto" employs strophic variation and a series of contrasting ritornelli. Each segment is for a new instrumental combination. The composer's suggested ornamentation indicates the types of improvisation possible and the virtuoso vocal technique of the period.

Scores

SSHS 1, 169–179

SSMS, 144–151

Act IV—The scene in which Orfeo disobeys Pluto's condition and Euridice is taken back to Hades illustrates recitative style and the affective use of dissonance.

Score

HAM 2, 7–9

Claudio Monteverdi, L'incoronazione di Poppea, Act 1, scene 3

Style features

This scene shows recitative, bel canto, and florid styles of singing. Although the styles tend to flow together, the tendency toward separation of the operatic aria into a self-contained number with a distinct structure is indicated by the momentary use of strophic variation-like sections.

Scores

* EMH, 364–372

* NAWM 1, 371–379

Claudio Monteverdi, "Ohimè dov' e il mio ben"

Style features

This duet illustrates trio texture and strophic variation on the romanesca.

Scores

* NAWM 1, 324–332

SSHS 1, 164–169

Lodovico Grossi da Viadana (ca. 1560–1627), "O Domine Jesu Christe"

Style features

This piece from *Cento concerti ecclesiastici* combines the modern monodic texture with prima prattica harmony.

Score

* NAWM 1, 451–452

Francesca Caccini (1587–ca. 1630), "Laudate Dominum"

Style features

Called "motetto" by the composer, this piece applies the monodic scoring to the free, sectional form inherited from the sixteenth-century motet; it would also have been designated sacred concerto. The text is that of Psalm 150, which speaks of praising God with music, and the vocal style suits these words with considerable ornamentation.

Score

HAMW, 22–30

Heinrich Schütz (1585–1672), "Saul, Saul, was verfolgst du mich"

Style features

This is an elaborate sacred concerto showing the extension of the Venetian style. The scoring includes two four-part choirs, six vocal soloists, two concertato violins, and continuo. The style of Gabrieli prevails in the choral ritornello sections, while in the monodic and duet passages the seconda prattica of Monteverdi allows for stronger affective expression.

Scores

   * EMH, 336–347

   HAM 2, 36–39

   * NAWM 1, 469–479

Giacomo Carissimi (1605–1647), Jephte

Style features

     Carissimi's best-known work, *Jephte* illustrates the techniques and full range of musical styles available in the early oratorio. The final choral lament is highly affective due to its double suspensions and the use of the descending tetrachord gesture. The source of the story is Judges 11.

Scores

   * EMH, 372–384—two excerpts with contrasting affections, but not the final chorus

   * NAWM 1, 457–468—Jephte's daughter's final aria and the concluding chorus

   SSHS 1, 256–263—the entire "second act" of the oratorio

   SSMS, 166–171—Jephte's daughter's final aria and the concluding chorus

Samuel Scheidt (1587–1654), Chorale partita on "Gelobet seist du, Jesu Christ"

Style features

     Scheidt's variations use scorings for from two to four parts. The chorale melody appears in various voices, sometimes ornamented. A number of contrasting styles and textures are employed.

Scores

   SSHS 1, 314–317

   SSMS, 160–163

Johann Jacob Froberger (1616–1667), Suite in E minor

Style features

The four dances are presented in standard order—allemande, courante, sarabande, gigue. There is a suggestion of the application of the variation principle in the allemande and courante. Each movement is a binary form in E minor, but there are three different treatments of the midpoint—cadence on B, half-cadence on B, and cadence on G.

Score

  * MM, 145–151

SAMPLE TEST QUESTIONS

Multiple Choice

1. In the middle of the seventeenth century the musical scholar
    _____ grouped the musical styles of the time into three
    classifications.

    A. Lodovico Grossi da Viadana
    B. Claudio Monteverdi
    C. Johann Jacob Froberger
    D. Heinrich Schutz
    E. Marco Scacchi

2. _____ included all types of early Baroque vocal music
    except sacred music and opera.

    A. stylus cubicularis
    B. stylus ecclesiasticus
    C. stylus gravis
    D. stylus theatralis
    E. strophic variations

3. The first opera was composed primarily by _____.

    A. Giulio Caccini
    B. Maria de' Medici
    C. Claudio Monteverdi
    D. Jacopo Peri
    E. Alessandro Striggio

4. The first public opera house opened in _____ in 1637.

    A. Florence
    B. Hamburg

    C. Mantua
    D. Rome
    E. Venice

5. The musical structure in which free material unfolds over a repeating bass formula is called _____.

    A. stylus cubicularis
    B. strophic variation
    C. stile moderno
    D. trio texture
    E. partita

6. The German composer _____ traveled to Venice to become acquainted with the music of Giovanni Gabrieli and Monteverdi.

    A. Froberger
    B. Gombert
    C. Scheidt
    D. Schein
    E. Schütz

7. Giacomo Carissimi is regarded as the composer most responsible for the development of the _____.

    A. sacred concerto
    B. oratorio
    C. suite
    D. strophic variation
    E. seconda prattica

8. The instrumental genre known as the _____ arose when the Renaissance canzona became fragmented into separate sections or movements.

    A. cantata
    B. ricercar
    C. romanesca
    D. sonata
    E. suite

9. In the seventeenth century a partita was a(n) _____.

    A. oratorio in one movement
    B. extended trio sonata
    C. set of variations
    D. improvisatory keyboard piece
    E. exposition

10. The first dance movement in a Baroque suite was most commonly a(n) _____.

    A. allemande
    B. ballet
    C. courante
    D. prelude
    E. recitative

True-False/Justification

1. The three-part division of musical styles in the seventeenth century did not explicitly include instrumental music.

2. The invention of opera around 1600 was the first time music had been employed in a dramatic context.

3. Because of its ecclesiastical position Rome did not become involved in the development of opera.

4. The term "bel canto" in the seventeenth century referred to a florid, virtuosic style of singing.

5. Monteverdi used the term "stile concitato" to designate any use of contrasting instrumental timbres for contrasting musical functions.

6. In the early seventeenth century the terms "aria" and "cantata" might have been used to refer to the same piece.

7. Claudio Monteverdi composed madrigals, songs with continuo accompaniment, and operas, but he never worked in the field of church music.

8. The "testo" was a university examination required of all student composers in seventeenth-century Italy.

9. Trio texture in the Baroque could employ four performers.

10. A chorale partita was one part of a four-part chorale setting.

Short Essay

Explain what is meant by "trio texture" in seventeenth-century music and why it was particularly attractive to musicians.

In a brief essay, explain how some of the same tendencies that guided the evolution of Renaissance vocal types into Baroque vocal chamber music genres operated in parallel fashion in instrumental genres during the period.

ANSWERS TO TEST QUESTIONS

Multiple Choice

1. E   Marco Scacchi
2. A   stylus cubicularis
3. D   Jacopo Peri
4. E   Venice
5. B   strophic variation
6. E   Schütz
7. B   oratorio
8. D   sonata
9. C   set of variations
10. A   allemande

True-False/Justification

1. T   Marco Scacchi seems to have been thinking of only music for voices in the church, chamber, and theater.

2. F   The Greek tragedy and medieval liturgical drama were sung, and the Renaissance had several types of staged and unstaged musical dramas.

3. F   Roman opera was influenced by the church in its subject matter.

4. F   Bel canto style used generally syllabic settings and relatively slow motion.

5. F   The stile concitato was a tremolo used to express an agitated affection.

6. T   Both aria and cantata could mean a strophic song.

7. F   Monteverdi wrote a great deal of sacred music and he served as maestro di cappella at St. Mark's in Venice from 1613 on.

8. F   The testo was one name for the narrator in an oratorio.

9. T   The trio in Baroque trio texture includes two melodic parts and a basso continuo for a melodic bass instrument and a chordal instrument.

10. F   A chorale partita was a set of variations on a chorale melody.

CHAPTER 14

THE HIGH BAROQUE

CHAPTER OVERVIEW

Opera in France developed in different ways from that in Italy in the seventeenth century. The character of the French musical scene arose from the strong centralization under the absolutist monarchy and the guidance of the Academie royale de musique, controlled by Jean-Baptiste Lully. In addition, the tradition of the court ballet influenced the opera. In Lully's mature operas or tragedies lyriques the French style matured. Vocal styles were not as differentiated as those in Italy, a typically French orchestra with five string parts was established, and the French overture was developed.

In England the native musical drama was the court masque; opera did not have a substantial place in England in the seventeenth century. Musical life in England was curtailed during the period of the Commonwealth. After the Restoration in 1660 music flourished again in both sacred and secular spheres. The outstanding composer of both types in this period was Henry Purcell.

Toward the end of the seventeenth century Italian opera attained a highly formalized structure in the opera seria. The opera was introduced by a three-movement sinfonia. The application of music to the drama relied on sharp distinctions between recitative, used for dialogue, and aria, which served for affective reflection. The da capo aria structure became standardized. Impressive virtuosity marked Italian singing, especially that of the castrati.

Among the most important musical ideas of North German music were those associated with Lutheran church music. Composers cultivated the sacred concerto and often incorporated the repertoire of chorales into it. Organists developed various styles and techniques of chorale setting for their instrument, the chorale prelude and chorale fantasia or fugue, as well as virtuosic freestyle pieces. The German music drama or Singspiel employed spoken dialogue rather than recitative and a less florid aria style than Italian opera.

Rapid progress was made in instrumental music during this period. Idiomatic styles for instruments, the concertato ideal, and terraced dynamics provided characteristic interest in instrumental music; the doctrine of affections justified its expressive value in the absence of words. In addition, composers began to explore the possibilities of large-scale structuring of instrumental music by means of key planning.

Fugue synthesized the imitative contrapuntal texture with harmonic planning. The construction of harmonically profiled subjects, the tonal answer, and the strong establishment of the home key at the end allowed adventurous harmonic exploration in the course of the piece.

Composers of suites expanded the number of dances by adding to the standard ones, and in the French they added characteristic titles. The harmonically structured binary form controlled all the standard dances.

The sonata for one or more instruments with basso continuo became the standard chamber-music genre in the seventeenth century. The trio sonata was particularly popular. The repertoire was classified into the sonata da chiesa and sonata da camera types, the latter essentially consisting of a set of movements like those of a suite. Arcangelo Corelli, the leading composer of sonatas, established the pattern for what became the standard principles of harmonic progression for the next two centuries.

The concerto arose from the application of contrasting large ensemble to the chamber texture of the sonata. In the concertos of Giuseppe Torelli harmonic departure and return and the alternation of free solo and ritornello material provided a successful structure for concerto movements. Antonio Vivaldi invented thematic material adapted to harmonic-structural function.

OBJECTIVES

1. To help the student understand how the social and political situations in France, England, Italy, and Germany produced corresponding musical ideas in the Baroque.

2. To familiarize the student with the various genres and styles of dramatic music in the different countries in the seventeenth century.

3. To acquaint the student with the important genres of instrumental music in the high Baroque.

4. To help the student understand the principles of musical structure developed during the seventeenth century.

TERMS, NAMES, AND CONCEPTS

Académie royale de musique
ballet de cour
Pierre Perrin
Jean-Baptiste Lully
Vingt-quatre violons du roi
comédie-ballet
Molière

tragédie lyrique
Philippe Quinault
air
French overture
masque
Henry Lawes
John Blow
Henry Purcell
semiopera
odes, welcome songs
fancy
Alessandro Scarlatti
Apostolo Zeno
opera seria
sinfonia simple recitative (secco recitative)
accompagnato recitative
arioso
da capo aria form
ritornello
castrati
Benedetto Marcello
continuo-Lied
Dieterich Buxtehude
Johann Pachelbel
chorale prelude
Vorimitation (fore-imitation)
chorale fantasia, chorale fugue
gebunden, frei
Singspiel
Reinhard Keiser
terraced dynamics
fugue
tonal answer
episode
stretto
pedal point
bourrée
gavotte
minuet
Johann Mattheson
Der vollkommene Capellmeister
ordre
Francois Couperin
L'art de toucher le clavecin
agréments
binary form
solo sonata
sonata da camera
sonata da chiesa
Arcangelo Corelli
Queen Christina of Sweden

Cardinal Pietro Ottoboni
concerto
Georg Muffat
concertino
tutti, ripieno
concerto grosso
solo concerto
ripieno concerto
Giuseppe Torelli
Antonio Vivaldi
Ospedale della Pietà

CLASROOM APPROACHES, ASSIGNMENTS, TOPICS FOR DISCUSSION

National Musical Traditions

Assign students to research and reconstruct the performance context, complete contents, and details of presentation of the music for each of the following: a French court ballet (e.g., the *Ballet de la nuit*), an English masque (e.g., *Comus*), a seventeenth or early-eighteenth-century German church service (i.e., in the churches where Buxtehude or J. S. Bach worked). Discuss with the class the effect of awareness of the original performance situation on the understanding of the music.

Opera

Have the class list differences between French and Italian operas in the late seventeenth century. They should include at least the following: content and structure of plot; name, scoring, and structure of the opening instrumental piece; singing styles; use of dance and chorus.
Assign the students to listen to a complete Baroque opera (*Dido and Aeneas* provides a good, concise example) and list the dramatic functions of each of the musical forces in late-seventeenth-century opera—solo singers, chorus, orchestra. When and how do their different types of musical numbers and styles of singing or playing (1) advance the drama, (2) express affective responses to dramatic situations, (3) "paint scenery," (3) provide musical diversion, (4) punctuate the dramatic structure? In the light of these observations discuss the conventions of high Baroque opera seria. Connect this conventionalism to Rationalist methods of thought.

Musical Structure

Diagram in class the structure of da capo aria by Alessandro Scarlatti and a solo concerto movement by Torelli in the same key. Students should recognize the similarity between the ritornello structure of the A section of the aria and the concerto movement. Discuss in what sense the aria might be thought of as a concerto movement for the singer and why the concerto movement might be considered an aria for the instrument.

Assign students to copy the subjects of a series of imitative pieces from the late sixteenth to the late seventeenth centuries. Play the subjects in class and discuss which more clearly fix a harmonic center and why. Examine some ritornello opening motives from Vivaldi's concertos and have students explain their effectiveness in establishing the key.

Assign students to compose a dance piece in binary form, using the style of the allemande, courante, sarabande, or gigue. A complicated texture is not necessary; they might score the composition in two lines only, either for keyboard or for melody instrument and basso continuo. Play the compositions in class. If they composed several different dances in the same key, the movements could be put together to form a dance suite.

MUSIC FOR STUDY

Jean-Baptiste Lully (1632–1687), **Alceste,** *Overture, excerpt from Act 2*

Style features

> The *Alceste* overture is clear example of the French overture structure. Performance practice issues include the use of *notes inégales.*

Score

> * NAWM 1, 385–387

Act II, scenes 7–8 illustrate characteristic French vocal styles in a short air and in recitative.

Score

> * EMH, 393–399

Henry Purcell (1659–1695), **Dido and Aeneas,** *conclusion*

Style features

> The introductory recitative establishes a sharply defined affect by means of descending semitones. Dido's lament employs a variant of the conventional lamento bass formula filled out with chromatic passing tones. The vocal style is bel canto. The aria illustrates Purcell's use of a ground bass to control the musical structure without binding the melodic phrasing to that of the ground.
>
> The concluding chorus uses madrigalistic melodic ideas and expressive "sighing" rests.

Scores

* EMH, 400–406

HAM 2, 144-145—recitative and aria only

* NAWM 1, 400–406

Henry Purcell, *Dido and Aeneas,* ed. Curtis Price (New York: Norton, 1986) gives a critical edition and a collection of essays and comments.

Alessandro Scarlatti (1660–1725), Griselda, *"Mi rivedi, o selva ombrosa"*

Style features

This aria provides a clear example of the da capo form, except for the omission of the opening ritornello at the return to the A section. The first vocal entrance illustrates the use of "motto" opening. The modulation in the A section is from C minor (written at the time with a signature of only two flats) to B flat, and the middle ritornello is extremely compact. The libretto is by Zeno.

Score

* NAWM 1, 412–415

Elisabeth-Claude Jacquet de la Guerre (ca. 1666–1729), Semele

Style features

This work is a cantata based on a classical myth. The work consists of an instrumental prelude and interludes for violin and continuo, recitatives, and three airs.

The airs are based on dancelike melodic ideas. The second is in gavotte style; the third is modeled on the minuet. Despite having the character of dances, these airs are not in the binary forms employed in dances but in a compact da capo form.

The inclusion of interpretative markings is noteworthy. The interlude following the second air is significantly marked "notes égales," indicating that *inégales* would be used by default.

Score

HAMW, 66–76

Arcangelo Corelli (1653–1713), Trio Sonata in E minor, op. 3, no. 7

Style features

Corelli's op. 3 sonatas are examples of the da chiesa type.

The first movement uses imitation between violins at the unison and with the bass at the octave. The cadence is effected by lowering the register and by rhythmic augmentation.

The fugal second movement includes the bass in the exposition. A real answer is used in the entrance of the second violin. Two characteristic Corellian chains of suspensions appear (meas. 30–31 and 47–49). There are stretto-like passages between the violins (meas. 35–36, 45–46). The final cadence echoes that of the first movement.

The beginning of the third movement illustrates a tonal answer. The movement uses a cadential hemiola as a written-out ritardando.

The final movement features dialogue between the the violins. A terraced dynamic change brings the sonata to a close.

Scores

* MM, 162–168

SSHS 1, 328–331

Giuseppe Torelli (1658–1709), Concerto for Violin, op. 8 no. 8, third movement

Style features

The structure is based on three ritornellos, the outer ones in the home key of C minor and the middle one in E flat. The solo violin plays with the ripieno first violins throughout the ritornellos; it and the continuo emerge from the ripieno sound at the beginnings of the solo sections. The style of violin writing is highly idiomatic, especially at the broken-chord passage over the pedal point in the second solo. A terraced dynamic change appears at the movement's end.

Scores

HAM 2, 126–129

* NAWM 1, 556–561

Antonio Vivaldi (1678–1741), Concerto Grosso in A minor, op. 3 no. 8, first movement

Style features

The ritornello material consists of several motivic elements, which function to establish the key, extend, and effect a strong cadence. (A complete statement of the cycle of fifths occurs in measures 5–9.) The structure is expanded from that of the Torellian ritornello form; the main internal ritornello is in D minor.

Score

HAM 2, 183–186—This compact score has the virtue of making very clear how the concertino instruments emerge from the ripieno group.

SAMPLE TEXT QUESTIONS

Multiple Choice

1. The dominant figure in music in seventeenth-century France was
   _____.

   A. François Couperin
   B. Jean-Baptiste Lully
   C. Jules Mazarin
   D. Georg Muffat
   E. Pierre Perrin

2. The leading musical entertainment at the French court in the first half of the seventeenth century was the _____.

   A. air de cour
   B. ballet
   C. concerto
   D. masque
   E. suite

3. The French opera overture had _____ main contrasting sections.

   A. 2
   B. 4
   C. 5
   D. 6
   E. 8

4. _____ developed a thoroughly rationalistic set of conventions for Italian opera seria around 1700.

   A. Arcangelo Corelli
   B. Jean-Baptiste Lully
   C. Alessandro Scarlatti
   D. Antonio Vivaldi
   E. Apostolo Zeno

5. Recitative supported by the entire ensemble of strings rather than only basso continuo is called _____.

   A. accompagnato
   B. arioso
   C. ripieno
   D. simple
   E. welcome song

6. A recurring orchestral passage called_____ might be used to unify the structures of both the large-scale Italian opera aria and the concerto movement.

   A. concerto grosso
   B. da capo
   C. exposition
   D. ritornello
   E. stretto

7. A(n) was_____ an organ work in which a chorale melody was employed in a single statement as a cantus firmus.

   A. chorale fantasia
   B. chorale prelude
   C. chorale partita
   D. church cantata
   E. concerto

8. Keyboard composers in _____ often included in their suites movements with characteristic titles rather than merely the names of dances.

   A. England
   B. France
   C. Germany
   D. Italy
   E. Spain

9. _____ means a passage of rapidly overlapping imitative entries of the subject, often used to increase the climactic effect at the end of a fugue.

   A. episode
   B. exposition
   C. pedal point
   D. stretto
   E. tonal answer

10. A sonata da chiesa was actually a _____.

   A. keyboard piece written on commission
   B. concerto for six instruments
   C. solo vocal piece for liturgical use
   D. prelude and fugue
   E. suite of dances

True-False/Justification

1. In the seventeenth century official academies were established to control the various disciplines in Italy.

2. French orchestral scoring in the Baroque period tended to be more dense than that of other countries.

3. The serious musico-dramatic works of Lully were not termed "opera seria" by the composer.

4. As they had in the case of the madrigal, English composers quickly imitated the Italian in the field of opera.

5. Henry Purcell's career led him to work in both secular and sacred music genres.

6. Sheer virtuosity and the demands of the singers were so important in the Italian opera that rationalism had no effect on the genre in the late seventeenth century.

7. The Italian opera opened with the same type of instrumental overture as did opera in France.

8. German organ music is called "free" when it does not depend on use of a chorale melody.

9. The fugue is the strictest form used in Baroque keyboard music.

10. A Baroque suite could be regarded as an exploration of a series of contrasting affections.

Short Essay

How did the social/political/cultural situations in different countries in the seventeenth century affect their musical traditions?

Explain the effect of harmonic planning in different genres of vocal and instrumental music in the high Baroque.

In what way did the doctrine of the affections contribute to the development of an aesthetic basis and to style in instrumental music in the seventeenth century?

ANSWERS TO SAMPLE TEST QUESTIONS

Multiple Choice

1. B   Jean-Baptiste Lully
2. B   ballet
3. A   2
4. E   Apostolo Zeno
5. A   accompagnato
6. D   ritornello
7. B   chorale prelude
8. B   France
9. D   stretto
10. E   suite of dances

True-False/Justification

1. F   The establishment of academies took place in France.

2. T   The standard French orchestration included five-part string writing.

3. T   Lully called his serious operas "tragédies lyriques."

4. F   The genre of opera was practically ignored by English composers in the seventeenth century.

5. T   Purcell held positions at both Westminster Abbey and the royal court.

6. F   Under Zeno the conventions of operatic structure were guided by rationalistic planning.

7. F   Italian operas were introduced by a three-part sinfonia rather than a two-part overture.

8. T   Organ pieces based on chorales are called *gebunden* or "bound."

9. F   Fugue is not a form but a set of procedures or techniques.

10. T   Johann Mattheson listed specific affections associated with the various dance types used in suites.

CHAPTER 15

THE END OF THE BAROQUE

CHAPTER OVERVIEW

As new musical ideas began to arise in the first half of the eighteenth century the styles and genres of Baroque music underwent their final brilliant phase of development.

George Frideric Handel made his mature career in England, appearing there first as a composer of Italian opera, for which he created a new vogue. His operas employ and exploit the conventions of the genre particularly effectively. At the end of the 1720s, however, the English audience abandoned the Italian opera for native, comic, ballad opera.

At the same time the Italians produced a comic operatic entertainment of their own in the intermezzo, staged between acts of the opera seria. The intermezzo took its plots from the commedia dell'arte and used the musical styles of serious opera, but on a smaller scale. It also reintroduced the bass voice, which had not been featured in Italian opera in the preceding generation.

The leading opera composer in France in the second third of the eighteenth century was Jean-Philippe Rameau. His operas became the target of attacks by musical conservatives who claimed that he had departed from the ideals of French opera established by Lully. The debate of the Lullistes and Ramistes was the first of a series of eighteenth-century critical battles over opera in France.

After he could no longer succeed in the field of opera, Handel turned to the oratorio, which, with their familiar biblical stories and text in the vernacular, held more appeal for the new middle-class audience in England. His oratorios combined his skill in opera with the great English choral-music tradition.

In Germany, besides the musicians of the noble courts, an important figure in musical life was the Kantor of commercial cities. The most successful of these music directors was Georg Philipp Telemann, who worked in Hamburg. Johann Sebastian Bach, after working in small-town churches and the courts of Weimar and Cothen, completed his career as Kantor in Leipzig. His works parallel his career, including church organ music, courtly ensemble music, teaching pieces, and sacred vocal music especially for the churches of Leipzig. In several composite works he assembled systematically organized collections of paradigmatic works in which he demonstrated the most sophisticated handling of Baroque genres and compositional techniques.

OBJECTIVES

1. To give the student an understanding of major developments in opera in the first half of the eighteenth century.

2. To acquaint the student with the reasons for the Handel's turn to the field of oratorio and the style of his works in that genre.

3. To help the student understand the phases of Bach's compositional career and his style.

TERMS, NAMES, AND CONCEPTS

George Frideric Handel
Royal Academy of Music
ballad opera
The Beggar's Opera
John Gay
Johann Christoph Pepusch
Nicola Porpora
Johann Adolf Hasse
Pietro Metastasio
intermezzo
commedia dell'arte
pasticcio
Giovanni Battista Pergolesi
La serva padrona
Jean-Philippe Rameau
Treatise on Harmony
La Pouplinière
Kantor
Georg Philipp Telemann
collegium musicum
Johann Kuhnau
Georg Böhm
Johann Adam Reinken
Johann Sebastian Bach
Orgel-Büchlein
Well-Tempered Clavier
Erdmann Neumeister
Picander (Christian Friedrich Henrici)
Clavierübung
B-minor Mass
Musical Offering
Art of Fugue

CLASSROOM APPROACHES, ASSIGNMENTS, TOPICS FOR DISCUSSION

Opera Styles in the First Half of the Eighteenth Century

Have students summarize in tabular form the characteristics of late Baroque Italian opera as illustrated by the operas of Handel, ballad opera, the intermezzo, French Baroque opera as illustrated by the works of Rameau. They should consider both libretto and music. Discuss in class the relationship between the styles of these genres and the audiences to whom each was addressed.

A useful research topic is a comparison of an Italian opera seria by Handel with one by Alessandro Scarlatti, or one by Rameau with one by Lully, showing the development of opera styles in each genre.

Musical Activities in the Eighteenth and Twentieth Centuries

Discuss the role of the Kantor in eighteenth-century Germany. How, if at all, is civic musical life supported and managed in modern America? What is the proper role of government in promoting music and the arts?

Compare the collegium musicum in Leipzig under Telemann and Bach to that in a modern college or university. How do they compare in terms of membership, audience, location and style of performances, repertoire?

Bach and Handel

In class, have students compare the careers, oeuvres, and styles of Bach and Handel. They should be able to explain what aspects of the two composers' careers motivated the differences between the genres in which they worked and their styles.

Discuss the ways in which Bach and Handel each encountered and absorbed the national styles of Italy and France. Do the students understand and find helpful Manfred Bukofzer's formulation that describes Handel's style as the coordination of national styles and Bach's as the fusion of national styles?

Possible topics for essay assignments are (1) comparison of the organ music of Bach and Handel, (2) the different meanings of "cantata" in their music, (3) Bach's and Handel's borrowings and parodies.

Discuss with students Bach's and Handel's careers and each man's responses to changing situations. How do they think a composer of Handel's temperament would work in the late twentieth century? Could a composer take the approach adopted by Bach?

Compare Bach's *St. Matthew* or *St. John Passion* to the musical treatment of the Passion story in the "rock opera" *Jesus Christ Superstar*. What are these works trying to express about the composers' and the times' understanding of the subject? How does each use contemporary conventions of musical style for dramatic expression?

Have students read the early criticism of Handel's *Messiah*, which attacked it as blasphemous for presenting the essence of the Christian faith as mere entertainment, in secular theaters, sung by theatrical singers. What legitimate boundaries exist between the sacred and secular in music? Compare these criticisms to early Christian and Reformation-period instances of concern about propriety in sacred music. Can the students think of similar concerns in twentieth-century America? How is *Messiah* itself perceived today? Since it is not a typical Handel oratorio, why has it become the most popular?

MUSIC FOR STUDY

George Frideric Handel (1685–1759), **Giulio Cesare,** *Act 2, scenes 1, 2*

Style features

This excerpt shows Handel's style in Italian recitative, followed by a scene based on the structure of a da capo aria. Handel extended the opening ritornello into an independent "sinfonia" to allow for the elaborate stage effect at the beginning of the scene and dispensed with the second ritornello (at meas. 90). The return to the A section begins at the first solo, in effect making this a "dal segno" aria structure. The interruptions of set musical numbers by recitative are an unusual concession to dramatic realism.

The standard rhythm of the sarabande helps to determine the affection.

Score

SSHS 1, 200–205

John Gay (1685–1732), **The Beggar's Opera,** *Act 2, scenes 1–3*

Style features

The first of the three songs in these scenes employs ternary form, the others use binary dance form. All are parodies, two from popular ballad tunes and one from Handel's opera *Rinaldo.* The songs are written on two staves, for vocal line and unfigured bass; they could be played and sung as they stand by a single player or performed with continuo realization.

Score

SSHS 1, 205–209

Giovanni Battista Pergolesi (1710–1736), **La serve padrona,** *duet "Lo conosco"*

Style features

> This duet serves as a miniature ensemble finale to act 1 of Pergolesi's famous intermezzo. The Italian comic convention of characters exchanging "Si" and "No" in an argument appears here. Pergolesi effectively set each item in Serpina's list of adjectives describing herself (meas. 30–39). Uberto's tendency to join Serpina in parallel sixths or tenths indicates that she begins to prevail.

Score

> HAM 2, 227–232

George Frideric Handel, **Israel in Egypt,** *nos. 3, 4, 5, 8*

Style features

> The description of the plagues of Egypt evoked some of Handel's most vivid pictorial writing. The chorus no. 4 has a particularly contorted fugue subject. The alto aria no. 5, illustrating the hopping of frogs, shows a considerable sense of humor. Harmony expresses the image of darkness in no. 8, which is also a fine example of choral recitative.

Score

> AAM, 256–269

Johann Sebastian Bach (1685–1750), Prelude and Fugue in D minor, **The Well-Tempered Clavier** *Book 1*

Style features

> The D-minor prelude exemplifies the perpetual-motion style. Its energy dissipates in the cadenzalike chain of diminished harmonies and the block chords at the end.
> The fugue has a subject with a very sharp melodic and rhythmic profile. In developing it, Bach employs inversion and stretto.

Scores

> * EMH, 555–559

> SSMS, 232–234—fugue only

Johann Sebastian Bach, Cantata no. 78, Jesu der du meine Seele

Style features

Bach composed the cantata—or, more correctly, sacred concerto—*Jesu der du meine Seele* for the fourteenth Sunday after Trinity in 1724. It illustrates the usual structure of a chorale cantata, expanding the typical six-movement model by the addition of the free duet "Wir eilen" following the first movement.

The opening chorus sets the first chorale verse as a cantus firmus in the soprano above affective material in the other parts. The movement is unified by the continual returns of the chromatically filled-in version of the chaconne bass pattern, affectively used to suggest lamentation.

The duet no. 2 illustrates trio texture and a walking bass. It follows da capo structure (with no middle ritornello).

The following recitative shows Bach's characteristically angular style of recitative. At its end the rhythm becomes measured by the regular eighth notes in the bass and there is an expressive melisma on "erzürnet" (angered).

No. 4, a tenor aria with obbligato flute, is laid out like the A section of a da capo aria. (The second solo section has the second half of the two-part text, which would in a full da capo aria appear in the B section.)

The recitative no. 5 is a good example of accompagnato recitative and of the use of arioso style at the end of a recitative movement.

The bass aria is scored for obbligato oboe with strings and continuo. Its approach to the form of the text resembles that of no. 4.

The chorale returns in four-voice cantional texture to conclude the work.

Scores

AAM, 212–245

* EMH, 514–546—recording includes only nos. 1, 3, 4

SSHS 1, 273–293

SSMS, 237–266

SAMPLE TEST QUESTIONS

Multiple Choice

1. Handel spent most of his early twenties in _____ where he mastered the musical style of that country.

   A. Austria
   B. England
   C. France
   D. Germany
   E. Italy

2. In his early years in London, Handel wrote many popular works in the genre of _____, which had not been explored to any great extent by English Baroque composers.

   A. anthem
   B. concerto
   C. dance suite
   D. opera seria
   E. trio sonata

3. *The Beggar's Opera* was the first work in a newly created genre, _____.

   A. ballad opera
   B. commedia dell'arte
   C. intermezzo
   D. oratorio
   E. passion

4. Pietro Metastasio made his greatest contribution to the history of music as a(n) _____.

   A. church musician
   B. virtuoso violinist
   C. opera librettist
   D. music patron
   E. Kantor

5. The intermezzo took its plots from the _____ which had been popular for a long time in Italy.

   A. opera seria
   B. commedia dell'arte
   C. pastoral
   D. oratorio
   E. tragédie lyrique

6. When Handel gave up composing operas he turned instead to the
   _____.

   A. ballad opera
   B. intermezzo
   C. oratorio
   D. suite
   E. trio sonata

7. Handel's oratorios are structured in _____ parts or acts.

   A. 2
   B. 3
   C. 4
   D. 5
   E. 6

8. Georg Philipp Telemann worked in the city of Hamburg as a(n)
   _____.

   A. music teacher
   B. maestro de cappella
   C. Kantor
   D. collegium musicum
   E. opera director

9. As concert master at the court in Weimar, Bach became familiar
   with the style of _____.

   A. English anthems
   B. French opera
   C. German organ chorales
   D. Italian sonatas and concertos
   E. Prussian court music

10. One of Bach's greatest achievements was his composition of
    _____ for performance in Leipzig church services .

    A. oratorios
    B. sacred concertos
    C. chorale melodies
    D. the B-minor Mass
    E. the *Musical Offering*

True-False/Justification

1. Italian opera was not only successful in its native area but also
   spread to other parts of Europe.

2. Handel abandoned the da capo aria structure in his works.

3. Parody was an important technique for creating music in the eighteenth century.

4. Italian opera audiences regarded the bass voice as appropriate to serious opera but not to comedy.

5. Alexandre-Jean-Joseph Le Riche de la Pouplinière made his greatest contribution to the history of music as an opera librettist.

6. French opera critics engaged in several heated arguments about the style of their national opera during the course of the eighteenth century.

7. Handel's oratorios are examples of oratorio volgare.

8. Bach never wrote an opera.

9. Because he did not travel beyond a fairly small portion of Germany, Bach did not come under the influence of styles from other countries.

10. Bach's *Musical Offering* was dedicated to the Leipzig city council to show the composer's gratitude for their support of the city's music program.

Short Essay

Explain what features of Handel's oratorios contributed to his success in that genre, and why.

Describe three different ways in which prominent composers of the late Baroque period earned their livelihoods and how those careers guided their output and styles.

ANSWERS TO SAMPLE TEST QUESTIONS

Multiple Choice

1. E   Italy
2. D   opera seria
3. A   ballad opera
4. C   opera librettist
5. B   commedia dell'arte
6. C   oratorio
7. B   3
8. C   Kantor
9. D   Italian sonatas and concertos
10. B   sacred concertos

True-False/Justification

1. T   Italian opera became popular in England and the German-speaking countries.

2. F   Handel employed the da capo form frequently in both operas and oratorios, sometimes with modifications for dramatic purposes.

3. T   Bach and Handel both used the device of parody, and the songs in *The Beggar's Opera* were parodies of well-known melodies.

4. F   The Italians used the bass voice in the intermezzo rather than in opera seria.

5. F   La Pouplinière was an important patron of music and the other arts.

6. T   Rameau's operas were the subject of such debate.

7. T   One reason for the appeal of the oratorios to the English was their use of the English language.

8. T   The duties of Bach's various positions did not call for the composition of operas.

9. T   Bach absorbed both French and Italian styles.

10. F   The *Musical Offering* was dedicated to King Frederick the Great of Prussia to commemorate Bach's visit to the court.

CHAPTER 16

NEW CURRENTS IN THE EARLY EIGHTEENTH CENTURY

CHAPTER OVERVIEW

During the course of the Baroque period the harmonic syntax of the common practice was established. In 1722 Rameau's *Traité de l'harmonie* articulated the principles and the procedures of functional tonality. This development provided an important foundation for the music of the eighteenth and nineteenth centuries.

An aesthetic move away from the grandiloquence of Baroque music took place in the galant style. The galant stressed charm and grace, lightness of texture, and rhythmic flexibility. The keyboard works of Domenico Scarlatti illustrate the style.

In France and Italy comic opera genres began to thrive in the first half of the eighteenth century. The opera buffa employed the same musical and theatrical conventions as the intermezzo but was independent from serious opera performances. In the Guerre des bouffons the French debated the merits of the Italian style, which they regarded as a challenge to their own taste. They also developed a native comic opera genre, the opera comique.

In Germany the Baroque gave way to the empfindsamer Stil, which was based on sentimental expression and flexibly changing emotions. This style is well expressed in the music of C.P.E. Bach and took advantage of the dynamic nuances of the piano.

Form takes on a special significance in the instrumental music of the eighteenth century. Of particular interest to composers was the binary form of Baroque dances. The addition of thematic events to articulate the tonal structure led to the important rounded binary structure.

In orchestral music the independent sinfonia began to take the place of the concerto grosso. Italian composers, especially in Milan, pioneered in the genre, basing their works on the three-movement opera sinfonia. In Germany the Mannheim composers expanded the sinfonia to four movements by regularly adding a minuet, and developed new approaches to orchestration and dynamic expression.

OBJECTIVES

1. To help the student understand the nature and significance of the appearance of the system of functional tonality.

2. To introduce the student to the new aesthetic principles of flexible style and expression in the galant and empfindsam styles that superseded the rhetorical aesthetic of Baroque music.

3. To acquaint the student with the new developments in mideighteenth-century Italian and French comic opera and the rivalry between Italian and French operatic taste in the middle of this period.

4. To give the student an understanding of the development of binary forms in the early eighteenth century.

5. To introduce the student to the early eighteenth-century independent orchestral sinfonia.

TERMS, NAMES, AND CONCEPTS

Traité de l'harmonie
functional harmony
    triad
    inversion
    root
    tonic, dominant, subdominant
    modulation
galant style
rococo
Johann Joachim Quantz
Versuch einer Anweisung die Flöte traversière zu spielen
Domenico Scarlatti
opera buffa
Guerre des bouffons
Jean-Jacques Rousseau
opéra comique
Empfindsamkeit, empfindsamer Stil
Carl Philipp Emanuel Bach
Versuch über die wahre Art das Clavier zu spielen
Frederick the Great
Charles Burney
Bartolomeo Cristofori
fortepiano
Gottfried Silbermann
First Berlin School
Sturm und Drang
rounded binary form
sinfonia
Giovanni Battista Sammartini
Mannheim
Johann Stamitz
"Mannheim steamroller"
"Mannheim rocket"

CLASSROOM APPROACHES, ASSIGNMENTS, TOPICS FOR DISCUSSION

Tonality and Form

Ask students to compare the principle of tonal harmony to principles that effect control in other contexts.

In what way do the conventions of word order in English sentence structures resemble the conventions of harmonic progression in the tonal system? How do departures from conventional ordering serve creativity in expression in language and in music? How does this compare to languages in which word order is less important in determining meaning?

How does the effect of tonality resemble the force of gravity? Does the expression "What goes up must come down" apply to music? Is tonality a product of natural law, or is it a human creation?

Discuss the relation of harmonic function to musical form at all levels. How does the sense of broad harmonic motion relate to the trend toward opposition or balance between short successive phrases as compared to a style that relies on spinning out figurations? Why was melodic articulation of movement structures (as in ritornello or variation forms) superseded by harmonic designs for form (as in binary and later sonata form) after the formulation of a theory of harmonic function?

National Styles

Hold a debate in class based on the arguments in the Guerre des bouffons, one group of students taking the pro-French side and another group the pro-Italian side. Students will want to do some outside reading on the issues. The arguments should be illustrated by critical commentary on specific representative musical examples. Alternatively, stage a similar debate on the relative merits of two contrasting recent popular styles (e.g., country-western vs. heavy metal).

Have students create a table showing the differences and similarities between the galant style and empfindsamer Stil in regard to scoring, dynamics, rhythm, melodic character, harmony, texture, form. They should recognize that both depended on greater flexibility of expression than was characteristic of Baroque music.

MUSIC FOR STUDY

Domenico Scarlatti (1685–1757), Sonata in D, K. 119

Style features

The motivic material in this sonata is clearly adapted to structural functions. The opening motive instantly establishes the tonality; the contrast material (meas. 36ff) has contrasting character and prolongs harmonic tension; the closing idea is strongly cadential (meas. 18ff, 73ff, 176ff).

The cluster-like dissonances used in the secondary-key material make a good effect on the harpsichord but not on the piano and provide a good example of how different the idioms of the two instruments can be.

A wide variety of textures and styles appears within this single, relatively compact piece. The virtuosic style features the agility idiomatic to the instrument.

The form is characteristic of Scarlatti's approach to the binary principle. The opening idea is quickly abandoned. After a cadenza-like arrival on V of V new material enters on the dominant minor, leading to a cadence in the dominant major to end the first part. The second part begins with new material and leads to an extended broken-chord statement of the original. The tonic is then introduced by the material formerly associated with the contrast key, and the remainder of the sonata is straightforwardly adapted by transposition from the first part.

Scores

* EMH, 564–570—This score and recording includes the Sonata in D minor K. 120, with which K. 119 may form a pair.

MCP, 25–34—also includes K. 120.

* NAWM 2, 1–4

Carl Philipp Emanuel Bach (1714–1788), Fantasia 1 in F (1785)

Style features

The dynamic and phrasing effects demand the fortepiano rather than the harpsichord. The dynamic indications pp, p, mf, f, ff appear, and extreme dynamic contrasts occur in immediate juxtaposition.

The opening and closing sections are unmetered. The middle section, though measured, exploits syncopations. The outer sections depend on figuration rather than melody; the figuration of the end is to be improvised by the player from the given right-hand notes and figured bass. In the central section there are many characteristic expressive gestures of the empfindsamer Stil.

A surprising range of harmonies appears. Some of the successions of harmonies are also employed for their shock value.

Texture is extremely varied.

Score

SSHS 2, 4–6

Johann Stamitz (1717–1757), Sinfonia in D major (La melodia germanica, op. 11, no. 3, 1754–1755), first movement

Style features

The sinfonia is scored for paired oboes (and/or flutes, clarinets) and horns, strings (about thirty players), and continuo instrument. The early sinfonia was often directed by the continuo player, though Stamitz led from the concertmaster's position. A variety of scorings is used. The oboes have prominent duet theme, introduced in meas. 51.

Dynamic markings used include p, f, ff, fp, cres, rinf. Two characteristic Mannheim crescendos appear in meas. 18–23 and 27–31.

The movement has no repeat and is not a clear derivative of binary form; the structure owes more to the Baroque concerto than to dance forms. On the small scale there is a very regular use of symmetrical phrasing.

Score

* NAWM 2, 42–50

SAMPLE TEST QUESTIONS

Multiple Choice

1. The first thorough formulation of the theory of tonal harmony is attributed to _____.

    A. Johann Sebastian Bach
    B. Carl Philipp Emanuel Bach
    C. Johann Joachim Quantz
    D. Jean-Philippe Rameau
    E. Johann Stamitz

2. To identify a triad, one has to classify a harmony not according to its sounding bass note but according to its _____.

    A. triad
    B. root
    C. inversion
    D. tonic
    E. modulation

3. The French term _____ describes music with such characteristics as elegance, grace, and charm.

    A. galant
    B. rococo
    C. essercizi

    D. Empfindsamkeit
    E. Guerre des bouffons

4. The Italian composer _____, a contemporary of Bach and Handel, spent most of his career in Portugal and Spain.

    A. Johann Joachim Quantz
    B. Jean-Jacques Rousseau
    C. Domenico Scarlatti
    D. Giovanni Battista Pergolesi
    E. Carl Philipp Emanuel Bach

5. The _____ was an independent genre of Italian comic opera that had many of the same traits as the intermezzo.

    A. opera buffa
    B. opéra comique
    C. Guerre des bouffons
    D. empfindsamer Stil
    E. Mannheim steamroller

6. An important center of development of the empfindsamer Stil was _____.

    A. Rome
    B. Paris
    C. London
    D. Vienna
    E. Berlin

7. The important treatise *Versuch über die wahre Art das Clavier zu spielen* (Essay on the true manner of playing the keyboard) was written by _____.

    A. King Frederick the Great
    B. Domenico Scarlatti
    C. Carl Philipp Emanuel Bach
    D. Johann Stamitz
    E. Jean-Jacques Rousseau

8. When the second part of a binary form reestablishes the tonic key with the material of the first part, adapted in such a way that no modulation takes place, the structure is called _____ binary form.

    A. galant
    B. principal
    C. tonic
    D. rounded
    E. sinfonia

9. After the Baroque period in music, the concerto was replaced as the
    leading genre of orchestral music by the _____.

    A. galant style
    B. dance suite
    C. Mannheim school
    D. fortepiano
    E. sinfonia

10. The famous Mannheim steamroller was actually a(n)
    _____.

    A. keyboard piece
    B. derivative of Baroque binary form
    C. nickname for Charles Burney
    D. orchestrated crescendo
    E. instrument invented in the eighteenth century

True-False/Justification

1. All music composed from 1600 to 1750 represents the Baroque
    aesthetic.

2. In the newer style of the eighteenth century the rate of harmonic
    change was slower than in Baroque music.

3. French opera comique resembled Italian opera buffa in using a very
    rapid, parlando style of recitative.

4. The most important Baroque musical form for future developments
    in the eighteenth century was the form used for dance music.

5. Characteristic of the newer styles of music in the eighteenth
    century was an unwillingness on the part of younger composers to
    bind themselves to insistent concentration on a single affection.

6. Rameau's theory insisted that harmony should always be derived
    from melody.

7. In the Guerre des bouffons the philosopher Jean-Jacques Rousseau
    was the main supporter of the French position.

8. The term *First Berlin School* identifies an important group of song
    composers in the mid-eighteenth century.

9. Johann Stamitz made his greatest contributions to music in the area
    of scoring.

10. The standard early-eighteenth-century Italian independent
    sinfonia generally had three movements.

Short Essay

How did national predilections and tastes manifest themselves in musical styles in the early eighteenth century?

How did new aesthetic and theoretical ideas affect musical structure from the phrase level to complete movement forms in the early eighteenth century?

ANSWERS TO SAMPLE TEST QUESTIONS

Multiple Choice

1. D Jean-Philippe Rameau
2. B root
3. A galant
4. C Domenico Scarlatti
5. A opera buffa
6. E Berlin
7. C Carl Philipp Emanuel Bach
8. D rounded
9. E sinfonia
10. D orchestrated crescendo

True-False/Justification

1. F New aesthetic viewpoints began to be expressed in music well before 1750.

2. T In the progressive style the harmony was more likely to change every measure than every beat.

3. F Opéra comique used not recitative but spoken dialogue.

4. T Binary dance form led to numerous significant variants in the eighteenth century.

5. T Flexibility of expressive style was a common trait in the music of many composers in the early eighteenth century.

6. F Rameau argued that melody should be derived from harmony.

7. F Rousseau favored Italian music.

8. T The First Berlin School composers produced songs for the German middle-class market.

9. T Stamitz was responsible for the development of new techniques of orchestration.

10. T   The independent sinfonia came from the three-movement opera sinfonia and only later gained the minuet as a fourth movement.

CHAPTER 17

THE EARLY CLASSIC PERIOD

CHAPTER OVERVIEW

The music of the Classic period developed within the context of the Enlightenment. It shares with the other arts of the time a tendency toward Apollonian objectivity and values such as symmetry, balance, and order.

Musicians in the second half of the eighteenth century generally still worked under the system of patronage, though the rise of the middle class began to affect the musician's life through the appearance of public concerts and the growth of music publishing. Of the two greatest masters of the period, Franz Joseph Haydn was highly successful under the patronage system, but Wolfgang Amadeus Mozart was not.

Opera buffa became more sophisticated in the early Classic period under the influence of the librettist Carlo Goldoni. The young Mozart showed particular talent in all the operatic genres. Serious opera was reformed to make the drama more important than the music and the style more simple and natural. Particularly significant for the reform of opera was Christoph Willibald Gluck, whose style caught on with special success in France.

Instrumental works were generally guided in the second half of the eighteenth century by the sonata plan, made up of movements in contrasting styles but linked by key. The most important genres were symphonies, string quartets and other chamber music, keyboard sonatas, concertos and sinfonie concertante, and divertimentos.

Of special importance was the development of the sonata form, an expansion of the rounded binary form. The Classic sonata form has two parts, each subdivided into two sections, based on a tonal plan of stability, contrast, tension, and resolution. The tonal structure is expressed by thematic events. The form was most commonly used for first movements of sonataplan works; certain modifications of it appear in slow movements, finales, and concertos.

The affective styles of the Baroque were adapted for use in the Classic period. In addition to creating changing emotional expression within pieces, they also suited the different functions of the sections within Classic musical structure.

OBJECTIVES

1. To help the student place the music of the Classic period in the context of the Enlightenment and the other arts of the time.

2. To acquaint the student with the social and economic environment in which Classic music developed.

3. To give the student an understanding of the aesthetics and styles of opera and the opera reform movement in the second half of the eighteenth century.

4. To help the student understand the conventions of musical structure and expression in Classic music.

TERMS, NAMES, AND CONCEPTS

Enlightenment
Classic
Johann Joachim Winckelmann
Vienna
Salzburg
academies
Johann Christian Bach
Karl Friedrich Abel
François-Joseph Gossec
Concerts spirituels
Johann Adam Hiller
Gewandhaus Concerts
Kenner, Liebhaber
Franz Joseph Haydn
Wolfgang Amadeus Mozart
Esterhazy family, Esterhaza
baryton
Leopold Mozart
Niccolo Piccinni
Padre Giovanni Battista Martini
Hieronymus Colloredo
Carlo Goldoni
dramma giocoso
opera reform
Christoph Willibald Gluck
Raniero Calzabigi
    Orfeo ed Euridice
    Alceste
sonata plan
symphony
minuet and trio
string quartet
Luigi Tomasini

piano sonata
sinfonia concertante
piano concerto
divertimento
    Serenade, Serenata, Nachtmusik
    Cassation
sonata form (sonata-allegro form)
    fantasy
exposition, development, recapitulation
sonata-rondo
concerto sonata form
    cadenza

CLASSROOM APPROACHES, ASSIGNMENTS, TOPICS FOR DISCUSSION

Enlightenment and Classicism

In class discussion, compare the values of Rationalism and the Enlightenment. Students should distinguish between the movements' emphases on idealism and practicality, reflection and experience, etc. Compare similarly the music of the Baroque and Classic periods. Contrast affect and emotion, passion and control, etc.

Classic Music in Its Social Context

Assign students to research the daily routine of a musician working in a noble court in the late eighteenth century. They should try to discover the details of the musician's day-to-day life such as housing, clothing, food. What duties, musical and otherwise, did the musician have to perform? What skills were required, and how were they learned?

Have students perform in class some examples of the middle-class music of the late eighteenth century, such as songs and simple keyboard pieces. Discuss how the music was circulated. Where, by whom, and for whom was it performed? What aspects of its style made it particularly suited to its social context?

Opera

Show in class a film or videotape of a performance of one of Gluck's operas. Discuss the elements of the stage design, costuming, and acting that reflect Classic ideals. Compare these to the style of the music.

Form and Expression in Instrumental Genres

Students may be able to compose a short movement in sonata form or one of its modifications. Given a key and a scoring, they may be able to work together in groups, choosing general styles for the various thematic and nonthematic segments of the form, then each composing a section (P, t, S, K, "fantasy"). Understanding of structural functions and the choice of styles is more important than artistic merit; humor should be encouraged. Students should mark the important segments of the structure of their movement, indicating both thematic and tonal plan. Discuss in class the value of convention in the Classic form and style.

Assign students to construct a concerto movement in the early Classic style for keyboard and strings, based on an early Classic keyboard sonata. If the students do not have time or expertise to write a full score, they should indicate what music would have to be added to the existing keyboard score and what its character and tonal plan would be.

MUSIC FOR STUDY

Christoph Willibald Gluck (1714–1787), Orfeo ed Euridice, *act 2, scene 1, excerpt*

Style features

This scene may be effectively compared to the parallel scene including "Possente sprito" in Monteverdi's *Orfeo*.

The example is scored for two instrumental ensembles, representing Hades and the approaching Orpheus, respectively.

The empfindsamer Stil expresses the horrors of Hades in the opening dance. Diminished-seventh harmonies appear throughout the scene, including at the imitation of the threefold barks of the three-headed Cerberus in the infernal choruses.

Orpheus's music represents the ideal of Classic control and simplicity.

Scores

* NAWM 2, 17–199

SSHS 2, 97–107 includes a slightly longer excerpt.

Franz Joseph Haydn (173–1809), Symphony No. 49 in F minor ("La passione"), second movement

Style features

This work illustrates the early Classic style in the symphony, before the conventions of the High Classic style had been consolidated, and the so-called Sturm und Drang in Haydn' s music. Although a second movement, this is a fast movement in sonata form. The scoring also illustrates a representative early Classic orchestra—two oboes, a bassoon to double the bass line in some passages, two horns, strings, and keyboard to play continuo.

Score

MCP, 95–108

Wolfgang Amadeus Mozart (1756–1791), Piano Sonata in D major, K. 284, first movement

Style features

The movement provides a good example of Mozart' s approach to the sonata form. Noteworthy is the considerable wealth of thematic and nonthematic ideas, including a multiplicity of clearly identifiable styles. Section 3 (the "fantasy") has the pedagogical advantage of being notably nonthematic; i.e., not a "development" of the main themes of the first part.

Score

AMSS, 206–211

Maria Theresia von Paradis (1759–1824), "Morgenlied eines armen Mannes" (1786)

Style features

The song shows a rather sophisticated approach to the genre. It clearly belongs to the highly cultured Viennese drawing room rather than to the North German burgher's home . The text represents a characteristic style, a somewhat sentimental portrayal of nobility in the lower class.

This is a strophic song in four stanzas; the form of the stanza is quite original. The vocal line departs in style from the ideal of *Volkstümlichkeit,* and in fact seems more Italianate and quasi-operatic than Liedlike. The piano accompaniment consists of a variety of idiomatic figurations, and there is a substantial solo interlude for the keyboard in the middle of each stanza.

Score

HAMW, 94–98

SAMPLE TEST QUESTIONS

Multiple Choice

1. The cultural movement into which the music of the second half of the eighteenth century must be placed is _____.

    A. Classical antiquity
    B. the Baroque

   C. Rationalism
   D. the Dark Ages
   E. the Enlightenment

2. An "academy" in the late eighteenth century was a common name
   for a(n) _____.

   A. opera comique
   B. amateur performance in a middle-class home
   C. concert in a public hall
   D. music course in a university
   E. marionette theatre

3. The term *Kenner* in the eighteenth century in Germany was used to
   identify a musical _____.

   A. toy
   B. expert
   C. instrument descended from the kithara
   D. school
   E. work for string quartet

4. Nicholas Esterhazy gained their prominence in music history as a
   result of his _____.

   A. music written for the Mannheim court
   B. excellent fortepianos manufactured in the 1770s
   C. musical patronage
   D. writings on musical life in the Classic period
   E. theoretical treatises

5. *Dramma giocoso* was a product of increasing sophistication in the
   _____.

   A. sinfonia concertante
   B. French court
   C. Singspiel
   D. baryton
   E. opera buffa

6. The principles of the reform of opera in the Classic period were
   outlined by _____ in the preface to his opera *Alceste* in
   1767.

   A. Johann Christian Bach
   B. Christoph Willibald Gluck
   C. Franz Joseph Haydn
   D. Wolfgang Amadeus Mozart
   E. Alexander Pope

7. The usual number of movements for a string quartet in the Classic period was _____.

   A. 1
   B. 2
   C. 3
   D. 4
   E. 5

8. Works with such titles as "Serenata," "Nachtmusik," and "Cassation" belong to the general category often known as _____.

   A. symphony
   B. fortepiano sonata
   C. divertimento
   D. opera buffa
   E. minuet

9. The so-called sonata form of the Classic period developed from the earlier _____ form.

   A. minuet
   B. rounded binary
   C. rondo
   D. ritornello
   E. fugue

10. In the closing passage of a Classic concerto first movement, the soloist was usually called upon to improvise a(n) _____.

   A. allegro
   B. binary theme
   C. cadenza
   D. development
   E. exposition

True-False/Justification

1. The concept of a "classic" style in art generally embodies a type of thinking associated with the Greek cult of Dionysus.

2. Johann Christian Bach, the youngest son of Johann Sebastian Bach, had a dual career in music.

3. Leopold Mozart was important not only as the father of Wolfgang Amadeus Mozart but also in his own right as a player and the author of a treatise on keyboard playing.

4. Wolfgang Amadeus Mozart prospered under the patronage system that still supported music brilliantly during his lifetime.

5. Carlo Goldoni is most important in the history of music for his contributions to opera.

6. Raniero Calzabigi made significant contributions to the reform of opera seria in the second half of the eighteenth century.

7. Keyboard sonatas and concertos in the Classic period typically have fewer movements than symphonies.

8. The Classic violin and keyboard sonata evolved from the Baroque sonata for violin and basso continuo.

9. The Classic sinfonia concertante evolved from the Baroque concerto grosso.

10. A characteristic variant of sonata form used in slow movements arises from the use of two "fantasy" sections, one in the middle of the first part of the binary form.

Short Essay

In what way did music and musical life in the late eighteenth century reflect the growing economic importance of the commercial middle class?

Compare the structural roles of thematic and harmonic planning in a Classic symphony first movement with the roles of themes and keys in the form of the late Baroque concerto.

How did expression contribute to the very conventional musical style of the Classic period?

ANSWERS TO SAMPLE TEST QUESTIONS

Multiple Choice

1. E   the Enlightenment
2. C   concert in a public hall
3. B   expert
4. C   musical patronage
5. E   opera buffa
6. B   Christoph Willibald Gluck
7. D   4
8. C   divertimento
9. B   rounded binary
10. C   cadenza

True-False/Justification

1. F   "Classic" art and music belong to the Apollonian tradition.

2. T   J. C. Bach was both a composer and an impresario.

3. F   Leopold Mozart's treatise is on violin playing.

4. F   Mozart did not get along with his patron and was eventually thrown out.

5. T   He was the finest opera buffa librettist of his time.

6. T   He worked as librettist for Gluck.

7. T   They usually have only three rather than four movements.

8. F   The Classic sonata for violin and piano arose from the addition of the violin to an essentially self-sufficient solo keyboard sonata.

9. T   The sinfonia concertante applies the form and style of the Classic period to the scoring of several solo players and ripieno group inherited from the Baroque.

10. F   The typical variant of sonata form in slow movements omits the "fantasy" passage altogether.

CHAPTER 18

THE HIGH CLASSIC PERIOD

CHAPTER OVERVIEW

The High Classic period is dominated by the figures of Haydn and Mozart. In 1781 Mozart was dismissed from his position and settled in Vienna. In the 1780s Haydn enjoyed a fully international reputation, and in the 1790s he became free to leave Esterhaza and traveled to England, where he had a brilliant success. During these two decades both men composed their greatest masterpieces and brought the Classic style to its peak.

Essential to the style was the creation of the dialoguelike, developmental texture, achieved in Haydn's string quartets and promptly adopted by Mozart. The texture suited the needs of the sonata form in ensemble music; it naturally affected the scoring of the symphony, in which it could be expanded to encompass the entire orchestra.

The concerto received its most significant development in the piano concertos of Mozart, written for his own use and for publication. These concertos attained integration of the solo part with the orchestral texture. In addition, the ritornello was fully integrated into the sonata structure.

Mozart's mature operas include opera seria, Singspiel, and opera buffa. The most important of these are the three comic operas in which Mozart collaborated with the librettist Lorenzo Da Ponte. In these works the composer adapted instrumental textures and the sonata structure to dramatic expression. In these three operas and in *Die Zauberflöte*, composed shortly before his death, Mozart dealt with current philosophical and social issues.

The entire aesthetic of the Classic style can be seen to differ decisively from that of the Baroque. The literary archetype for music in the Classic period is drama or the novel. Expression arises from the pattern of stability and instability, tension, climax, and resolution in musical form, coordinated with thematic materials of contrasting characters.

Beethoven came onto the musical scene just after Mozart's death. He spent his first decade there mastering the Classic style and establishing his reputation mainly as a pianist and composer for the piano. Already, however, his music showed his aggressive and rugged character.

Colonial America began to produce noteworthy composers during the revolutionary period. Among these, the most remarkable was William Billings of Boston. The popular American genres of the period include the fuging tune, songs, and battle pieces for keyboard. Some of the cities and the Moravian communities of Pennsylvania and North Carolina had more sophisticated musical culture based on the concert music of Europe.

OBJECTIVES

1. To help the student understand the position and achievements of Haydn and Mozart in the development of the High Classic style in instrumental music.

2. To acquaint the student with the musical-dramatic expression and the philosophical-social content of Mozart's late operas.

3. To help the student understand the way in which drama serves as the literary model for musical expression in Classic music.

4. To introduce the student to the music of Beethoven in his first period.

5. To give the student an understanding of the position and character of music and musical life in colonial and revolutionary America.

TERMS, NAMES, AND CONCEPTS

Johann Peter Salomon
Die Schöpfung
Gottfried van Swieten
Johann Wolfgang von Goethe
"conversational" texture
Janissary music
Lorenzo Da Ponte
    Le nozze di Fiaaro
    Don Giovanni
    Così fan tutte
Die Zauberflöte
Ludwig van Beethoven
Christian Gottlob Neefe
Ferdinand von Waldstein
Johann Schenk
Johann Georg Albrechtsberger
Antonio Salieri
Period of "Imitation"
fuging tune
William Billings
Moravian Brethren

Francis Hopkinson
battle piece
James Hewitt

CLASSROOM APPROACHES, ASSIGNMENTS, TOPICS FOR DISCUSSION

Developments in Classic Style

Be sure students understand the nature of the "conversational" texture in High Classic ensemble music. They should be able to distinguish this texture from counterpoint. Discuss the effect on the perception of the treatment of musical material; i.e., the concept of development of motives throughout the scoring. Draw attention to the way in which this treatment constitutes an integration among the different instrumental lines. Students should compare this integration to that achieved in the High Renaissance by the use of *fuga* in polyphonic vocal music .

Have students explain the difference between the application of the ritornello as a structural articulating device in the early Classic concerto and the integration of the ritornello into the sonata process in Mozart's mature concertos. Discuss the validity of the interpretation of the opening section as a "first exposition" rather than as a ritornello; is there a rationale for defining "exposition" as a presentation of thematic material rather than of tonal contrast? In regard to the integration of the ritornello into the sonata structure, have students evaluate the later tendency in performance practice to omit the solo player from the opening section of late Mozart concertos.

Compare the late orchestral works of Haydn and Mozart composed for large public audiences in Vienna, Paris, and London to those they composed earlier for court audiences in Salzburg and Esterhaza. What evidences do the late works show of the composers' concern for reaching an audience of *Liebhaber* rather than of *Kenner*?

Opera and Drama

Assign students to listen to Mozart's and Da Ponte's operas and *Die Zauberflöte* and to make a list of examples of different expressive styles in the music. Have them pay particular attention to which styles are assigned to which characters and sentiments. Are the more advanced and sophisticated or the more simple and immediately appealing styles generally associated with the more sympathetic characters? What does the use of particular styles for certain characters and situations suggest about the composer's attitude toward social liberalism and the decline of the aristocracy in European culture in his time?

Discuss in class the tendency of opera to adopt such instrumental procedures as sonatalike structures and motivic development in ensemble writing, and at the same time the tendency of instrumental works to take up dramatic styles and processes as their expressive model. Can students anticipate what aesthetic position this interchange of musical ideas between symphonic and operatic genres might be leading toward?

Early Beethoven

Assign students to read about the general cultural life of Bonn and of Vienna in the 1780s and 1790s. Discuss what role his growing up in Bonn played in shaping Beethoven's character, and why Vienna attracted the young composer. Have students identify which aspects of Viennese life and society seemed inimical to Beethoven in his first decade there.

American Music in the Eighteenth Century

Many eighteenth-century psalm settings and fuging tunes can be sung by students in class. Students should note that professional polish is not a necessary aesthetic goal in this music, and they should be encouraged to sing with commitment even if they are not vocally talented. Billings' "Chester" and "When Jesus Wept" stand as classics in early American literature, and it is worth the necessary class time to have students learn them.

MUSIC FOR STUDY

Franz Joseph Haydn, String Quartet in C major, op. 33, no. 3, first movement

Style features

Much of the thematic material in this movement is conceived motivically, and "conversational" or developmental texture appears in all the sections of the sonata form. In addition, the closing theme incorporates a rhythmic diminution of the P theme, lending additional integration to the structure. This relationship is made explicit at the beginning of the second half of the movement (meas. 60–74).

Score

SSHS 2, 18–23

Franz Joseph Haydn, Symphony No. 99 in E flat

Style features

The first movement employs the full Classic orchestra scoring, intended for the London orchestra. Its structure is that of a large-scale symphonic sonata form with a slow introduction in the empfindsam or sturm und Drang style. Students should note the proportions of the parts and sections of the form: Part l—section 1, meas. 1–71, and section 2, meas. 72–89; Part 2—section 3, meas. 90-137, and section 4, meas. 138–202. The motivic content of the movement should also be traced.

The second movement is a good example of the Haydn Adagio in a brief sonata form.

The minuet features a momentary canonic imitation at measures 12ff. The trio is in the unexpected remote key of C major.

The light-spirited finale is based on a principal rondo theme in closed binary form.

Score

MCP, 157–228

Wolfgang Amadeus Mozart, Piano Concerto in D minor, K. 466, first movement

Style features

The structure of the movement provides a good example of the concerto sonata form with the opening ritornello fully integrated into the thematic process.

The opening motivic material has an ominous, perhaps demonic quality, suggesting an affinity with *Don Giovanni*, which is in the same key. The solo has a new idea to introduce itself (meas. 77ff) and another associated with the secondary key area in the exposition (meas. 128ff).

Score

AAM, 340–364

Wolfgang Amadeus Mozart, Le nozze di Figaro, *opening scene*

Style features

The duet No. 1 illustrates the composer's use of music to indicate the contrasting actions and moods of the two characters, and demonstrates the ultimate resolution of the two moods into one as both singers take up Susanna's melody.

The recitative that follows will give students a good example of the style of eighteenth-century comic recitative.

The second duet employs change of key (to the relative minor) to reflect change of mood. The use of horns to symbolize a cuckold probably must be pointed out and explained to the students.

Score

SSHS 2, 108–116

Ludwig van Beethoven (1770–1827), Piano Sonata in C minor, op. 13 ("Pathétique"), first movement

Style features

The movement shows Beethoven's imitation of the styles of his Classic predecessors in the use of the empfindsamer stil in the opening, and the Mannheim steamroller in the P theme. The structure and texture clearly show how Beethoven synthesized his role as a piano performer with his desire for symphonic expression.

Score

* NS 1, 573–579

SAMPLE TEST QUESTIONS

Multiple Choice

1. After 1781 Mozart made his home in _____.

    A. Berlin
    B. London
    C. Mannheim
    D. Paris
    E. Vienna

2. The music patron Baron Gottfried van Swieten is important because he helped acquaint Viennese musicians and music lovers with _____.

    A. the Mannheim symphony style
    B. the works of Bach and Handel
    C. French music
    D. the art history of Winckelmann
    E. American fuging tunes

3. Haydn achieved the first notable successes with the "motivic-conversational" texture in his _____.

    A. symphonies of the 1790s
    B. baryton trios
    C. string quartets
    D. operatic recitatives
    E. late oratorios

4. Haydn's late symphonies were composed for performances in
    _____.

    A. the palace at Esterhaza
    B. England
    C. Paris
    D. Viennese concert halls
    E. none of the above

5. Many of Mozart's _____ were written for the composer
    himself to perform at public concerts.

    A. opera arias
    B. string quartets
    C. piano concertos
    D. fuging tunes
    E. none of the above

6. Lorenzo Da Ponte is important in the history of music for his work
    as a(n) _____.

    A. opera librettist
    B. music theorist
    C. innovator in the composition of string quartets
    D. critic
    E. impresario

7. Beethoven moved in 1792 from his home in Bonn to _____.

    A. Berlin
    B. London
    C. Paris
    D. Rome
    E. Vienna

8. Beethoven's performance instrument was the _____.

    A. flute
    B. trombone
    C. violin
    D. cello
    E. piano

9. An important composer of choral music in the period of the
    American Revolution was _____ of Boston, who gave up
    the craft of a tanner to become a musician.

    A. Johann Peter Salomon
    B. Francis Hopkinson
    C. William Billings

    D. James Hewitt
    E. Lorenzo Da Ponte

10. The model for musical expression in the Classic style is
    _____.

    A. mathematical proportions
    B. poetry
    C. oratory
    D. drama
    E. architectural symmetry

True-False/Justification

1. *Die Schöpfung* and *Die Jahreszeiten* are the nicknames of two of
   Haydn's last twelve symphonies.

2. The motivic-conversational texture was necessary to the invention
   of the sonata form.

3. Haydn's and Mozart's mature symphonies do not always use a full
   complement of paired wind instruments.

4. The style of the symphony changed in the Classic period due to the
   changing position of the genre in concert life.

5. One characteristic feature of the High Classic concerto is the
   integration of the ritornello with the sonata form.

6. Sonata form was a purely instrumental form and did not affect
   vocal music in the Classic period.

7. Mozart composed important examples of Singspiel as well as
   Italian operas.

8. The plots of some of Mozart's operas reflect social and
   philosophical issues of the time.

9. Because Beethoven was learning his craft by imitating his
   predecessors in his first decade in Vienna, there is no trace of his
   own personality in his music from that period.

10. The American fuging tune was a type of keyboard piece that
    illustrated battles and included fugues modeled on those of Johann
    Sebastian Bach.

Short Essay

Discuss several examples of ways in which compositional principles
developed in one musical genre influenced another in the High Classic
period.

Explain how economic and political trends, ideas, or events were reflected in music in the late eighteenth century.

ANSWERS TO SAMPLE TEST QUESTIONS

Multiple Choice

1. E   Vienna
2. B   the works of Bach and Handel
3. C   string quartets
4. B   England
5. C   piano concertos
6. A   opera librettist
7. E   Vienna
8. E   piano
9. C   William Billings
10. D drama

True-False/Justification

1. F   *The Creation* and *The Seasons* are late oratorios by Haydn.

2. F   The motivic-conversational texture was suited to the parts of sonata form that expressed instability, and it helped supply a high degree of integration to a sonata-form movement, but the form itself did not depend on it.

3. T   High Classic symphonies often call for only one flute, either oboes or clarinets but not both, and no trumpets.

4. T   The early Classic symphony was usually intended for the home of a wealthy aristocrat, but the later Classic symphony was more likely to be played for a middle-class audience in a large concert hall.

5. T   In Mozart's mature concertos the thematic material of the ritornello serves as the thematic material in the sonata plan.

6. F   Mozart employed some of the principles of sonata form in his operas.

7. T   *Die Entführung aus dem Serail* and *Die Zauberflöte* were both examples of Singspiel.

8. T   *Le nozze di Figaro* attacks the aristocracy, and *Die Zauberflöte* incorporates Masonic liberal ideas.

9. F   Beethoven's music in his period of imitation differs from that of his models in its forceful expression and boisterous humor.

10. F   The fuging tune was a choral piece that employed passages of polyphonic imitation.

CHAPTER 19

THE RISE OF THE ROMANTIC MOVEMENT

CHAPTER OVERVIEW

At the root of Romanticism was the emphasis on the rights of the individual that grew from the political philosophies of the Enlightenment. The Romantic period was consequently one of political revolutions. Social revolution also followed the Industrial Revolution. The stress on individualism led to an artistic interest in emotion and subjects that inspire emotion. The techniques of Romantic art depend on the opposition to assumptions that underlay Classicism. The two movements can be regarded as phases in a single development.

Beethoven became an important model for Romantic musicians and artists in general. He entered his own Romantic phase in 1802 with a new style based on the ideal of heroism. This characterized his personal life, including his coping with his deafness, as well as his musical style and his manner of composition. In his last period, 1815–1827, Beethoven turned inward. He became more introverted, and his musical projects were largely intense and experimental.

In the early Romantic period, Franz Schubert developed the Romantic Lied. He based his style on a synthesis of the principles of the folk-style Lied and of the ballad. His songs asserted a new role for the composer as interpreter of the poem.

In the nineteenth century, opera continued to dominate the musical scene in Italy, where the style moved only gradually away from that of Classicism. Opera in France was more progressive, strongly influenced by the revolution there. In Germany Carl Maria von Weber forged a truly Romantic opera style.

OBJECTIVES

1. To introduce the student to the ideals and stylistic traits of Romanticism.

2. To familiarize the student with the styles of Beethoven's middle and late periods.

3. To help the student understand the principles of the Romantic Lied.

4. To give the student an understanding of the contrast of national operatic styles in Italy, France, and Germany in the early nineteenth century.

TERMS, NAMES, AND CONCEPTS

Romanticism
E.T.A. Hoffmann
Period of "externalization," "Heroic" Period
Heiligenstadt Testament
rescue opera
Fidelio
character variation
Eroica Symphony
Symphony No. 5
Pastoral Symphony
song cycle
An die ferne Geliebte
Period of "reflection"
Missa Solemnis
Symphony No. 9, "Ode to Joy"
Second Berlin School
Karl Friedrich Zelter
ballad
Johann Rudolf Zumsteeg
Franz Schubert
modified strophic form
Die schöne Müllerin
Winterreise
Gioacchino Rossini
Luigi Cherubini
Carl Maria von Weber
Paris Conservatory

CLASSROOM APPROACHES, ASSIGNMENTS, TOPICS FOR DISCUSSION

Romanticism

Assign students to write a romantic poem or story or to draw a romantic picture. Discuss their works in class, drawing attention to the romantic qualities of the topics with which they choose to deal, as well as any characteristic romantic techniques they employ. Have students consider in what ways their own lives as young adults in the late twentieth century are affected by the subjects that inspired nineteenth-century Romantic artists—love, death, religion, patriotism, war, nature.

Have students bring to class works of literature or visual art that they feel demonstrate techniques of Romantic style. Let each student explain what techniques his or her chosen work illustrates.

Have students gather programs from orchestra concerts or lists of the operas performed in a season at a major opera house. They should observe that the major body of the repertoire performed on opera and concert stages in the twentieth century is still that of the Romantic period. In class discussion, have them consider what characteristics of life in the Romantic period still remain at the end of the twentieth century. Do they feel that the style of nineteenth-century music seems appropriate to express modern feelings and ideas? If not, why does Romantic music dominate the repertoire?

Beethoven

Have students consider whether Beethoven would be any less important in the history of music if we knew only his music and not about his life. Do his deafness, his affair with the "Immortal Beloved," his feelings about Napoleon and the noble aristocracy have an important effect on our understanding of his music? What about his struggles with composition as recorded in his sketchbooks?

Discuss with students the significance of Beethoven's late works. Do they properly belong to Romanticism? To some other movement? Is there a difference between the Ninth Symphony and the late string quartets in this respect?

Songs

Have students discuss what kind of poem makes a good song. How are the criteria different for a Classic song and a Romantic song? For a Lied and a ballad?

Compare settings of the same text by different composers—for example, one Second Berlin School composer's (Zelter's or Reichardt's), Schubert's, and Loewe's settings of Goethe's "Erlkönig." Students should consider the relative importance of the poet, the composer, and the performer in interpreting the text in each case.

Opera

Discuss with students the nonmusical concerns of the typical opera audience in the early nineteenth century in Italy, in France, and in Germany. What did each audience expect from the opera? How did the opera composer fulfill those expectations in each case?

Have students consider the staging of early-nineteenthcentury operas. What would be required for an Italian operatic comedy, a French postrevolutionary opera, a German Romantic opera? If possible, show students a film or videotape of an early Romantic opera in class, and discuss how the staging could be effected without electric lights or motors.

MUSIC FOR STUDY

Ludwig van Beethoven, Symphony No. 3 in E flat, "Eroica" (1802–1804)

Style features

Although externally the symphony follows the Classic plan, it is twice as long as the longest symphonies of the major Classic composers.

The first movement embodies the idea of heroism in its early destabilization of tonality (the surprising C-sharp diminished seventh chord at the end of the first phrase), of texture (motivic-conversational style), and of rhythm (syncopation). The instability continues throughout the movement, even in sections that were characteristically stable in Classic sonata form. The development section (section 3) is disproportionately long in comparison to the other sections of the form. Tonal stability and antecedent-consequent phrase structure arrive only late in the structure, producing a climactic ending after nearly continuous tension.

The slow movement is a funeral march in large ternary form. The style derives from that of the funeral marches of the French revolutionary period. The middle section of the form turns to the major key. The fragmented presentation of the theme at the end suggests that emotion interrupts the statement.

In the scherzo Beethoven expresses sheer energy. Noteworthy is the very high horn writing. The energy of the rhythm becomes so driving that it can be stopped only by a shift of meter.

The finale is a set of character variations, including some recollection of the funeral-march style.

Scores

ARM, 17–49

MCP, 640–819

* NAWM 2, 88–105—second movement only

Ludwig van Beethoven, String Quartet No. 14 in C-sharp minor (1825–1826)

Style features

The sound of the writing for the strings often exploits the different colors of their extreme registers.

Several contrasting expressive styles are suggested. The first movement uses fugal style and evokes a sense of religious reflection. The second and fifth movements, by contrast, employ a more "popular" style. The slow fourth movement is a set of character variations.

In spite of the work's division into seven movements, the model of the four-movement sonata plan is detectable, if one regards the first movement as a slow introduction and the third and sixth movements as transitions, interludes, or introductions to their following movements. The second movement is a compact sonata form, the fourth is in variation form, the fifth a scherzo (in style, though it is not in triple meter), and the final movement is a sonata form.

Scores

AAM, 432–441—first two movements only

ARM, 50–83

MCP, 886–927

* NAWM 2, 31–38—first two movements only

Franz Schubert (1798–1828), "Erlkönig," D. 328

Style features

This is a classic example of Schubert's assertively interpretive treatment of a poem. The piano and voice are clearly used to suggest the images, emotions, and sounds of the speakers. The galloping rhythm must be understood to exploit an image in Goethe's ballad that in both poem and music expresses emotional agitation. Harmony is treated interpretively in the use of minor and major keys and in the expression of rising excitement by a sequential upward modulation.

The form is a rondolike adaptation of the strophic folksong model.

Scores

ARM, 119–125

* NS 2,1–7

Franz Schubert, "Auf dem Wasser zu singen," D. 774

Style features

The accompaniment represents one of Schubert's many treatments of the image of water.

This song illustrates the use of strophic form. Students should consider how the singer is able to take advantage of the music to express emotions of different types in the different stanzas.

Score

ARM, 127–129

Gioacchino Rossini (1792–1828), Il barbiere di Siviglia, *"Una voce poco fa"*

Style features

The scoring shows Rossini's characteristically Italian inclination to keep the orchestra out of the way of the voice, as well as typical Rossinian orchestral material in the introduction and interlude. The melodic writing, while allowing for virtuosic display, is essentially vocal. The style still allows, like Baroque opera arias, for improvisation by the singer at the fermatas and repetitions. The structure has two parts—a romantic recitativelike introduction, followed by a fast aria reflecting Rosina's spirited character.

Score

* NAWM 2, 364–372

Carl Maria von Weber (1786–1826), Der Freischütz, *"Wolf's Glen" scene*

Style features

The orchestra clearly takes over the function of musical expression. Much of the scene is melodrama; i.e., spoken words with orchestral accompaniment.

The use of the diminished seventh chord to symbolize the mysterious or evil, very evident in this scene, soon became a cliché in later dramatic music.

Scores

MRP, 24–53

* NAWM 2, 458–493

SSHS 2, 256–269—piano-vocal score

SAMPLE TEST QUESTIONS

Multiple Choice

1. An important model for the success of a heroic personality in
    political life at the turn of the nineteenth century was
    _____.

    A. Jean-Jacques Rousseau
    B. Napoleon Bonaparte
    C. Robert Fulton
    D. Charles Darwin
    E. Karl Friedrich Zelter

2. Beethoven's middle period is sometimes known as his
    _____.

    A. heroic period
    B. period of imitation
    C. period of reflection
    D. pastoral period
    E. Second Berlin School

3. The Heiligenstadt Testament was Beethoven's _____.

    A. personal copy of the Bible
    B. Fifth Symphony
    C. reflection on his deafness and his vocation
    D. letter to the Immortal Beloved
    E. only opera

4. The poet who wrote the text Beethoven used in his Ninth
    Symphony was_____.

    A. Lord Byron
    B. Johann Wolfgang von Goethe
    C. E.T.A. Hoffmann
    D. Wilhelm Müller
    E. Friedrich Schiller

5. Two important examples of the _____ are *An die ferne
    Geliebte* and *Die schöne Müllerin.*

    A. ballad
    B. German Romantic opera
    C. song cycle
    D. aria di sorbetto
    E . escue opera

6. _____ combined the folk ideal in song with personal interpretation of the song text.

   A. Johann Wolfgang von Goethe
   B. Franz Schubert
   C. Carl Maria von Weber
   D. Karl Friedrich Zelter
   E. Johann Rudolf Zumsteeg

7. _____ was idealized by early Romantic opera librettists because he provided a model of a great artist who succeeded despite his disregard for standard rules of artistic form.

   A. William Blake
   B. Luigi Cherubini
   C. Alexander Pope
   D. William Shakespeare
   E. Walt Whitman

8. Italian opera composers in the early nineteenth century often used the process of _____ to recycle their music in order to keep up with the demand for new works.

   A. aria di sorbetto
   B. character variation
   C. organic unity
   D. parody
   E. reminiscence theme

9. The rescue opera was created in _____ around 1800.

   A. Austria
   B. England
   C. France
   D. Germany
   E. Italy

10. _____ never achieved much public acclaim and relied for his daily living on the generosity of his friends.

   A. Beethoven
   B. Cherubini
   C. Rossini
   D. Schubert
   E. Weber

True-False/Justification

1. The Romantic movement was closely linked to a new view of the place of people in society.

2. Romanticism placed a high value on fulfillment and satisfaction.

3. Continuity and asymmetry are important features of Romantic artistic style.

4. Classicism and Romanticism in music share a common model for musical expression.

5. Beethoven's late string quartets are highly intense, structurally and texturally complex, and not aimed at public appeal.

6. The songs of the Second Berlin School were well suited to the German middle-class music market.

7. To express the ideas in the poetry more effectively without abandoning the strophic model for his songs, Schubert used the character variation.

8. Because sherbet was a popular treat in Italy, the arias for the most important characters in an Italian opera were called *aria di sorbetto*.

9. The waltz became especially popular in Austria under Prince Metternich.

10. The modern music conservatory was established after the American Revolution in Philadelphia.

Short Essay

Describe several examples of organic connection in multimovement musical genres. Name specific works that illustrate this principle and explain how the organic unity occurs in each case.

Discuss the contributions to Romantic music of three different historical figures who were not musicians themselves.

ANSWERS TO SAMPLE TEST QUESTIONS

Multiple Choice

1. B   Napoleon Bonaparte
2. A   heroic period
3. C   reflection on his deafness and his vocation
4. E   Friedrich Schiller
5. C   song cycle
6. B   Franz Schubert
7. D   William Shakespeare
8. D   parody

9. C   France
10. D   Schubert

True-False/Justification

1. T   Romanticism depended on individual freedoms and differences.

2. F   In Romanticism, longing or yearning is more important than fulfillment.

3. T   Continuity and asymmetry thwart Classic expectations of articulation and balance, creating emotional response.

4. T   Both the Classic and Romantic styles are based on drama as the aesthetic model.

5. T   The late quartets of Beethoven embody the composer's period of reflection and private experimentation.

6. T   The Second Berlin School composers' songs were simple to perform and generally expressed intimate sentiments.

7. F   Schubert combined strophic form and freedom to express the text in modified strophic form.

8. F   The *aria di sorbetto* was an aria for a minor character, during which the audience might break for a snack.

9. T   The waltz suited the Viennese taste for light social entertainment after the political restabilization following the defeat of Napoleon.

10. F   The conservatory was founded in Paris in order to provide a way to train musicians after the end of the nobility and its musical patronage.

CHAPTER 20

THE MATURE ROMANTIC PERIOD

CHAPTER OVERVIEW

The composers who reached maturity in the second quarter of the nineteenth century represent the consolidation of the Romantic style. Characteristically, their lives included sources of income and activities other than composing. Their biographies are often intimately connected with their music, and several also wrote extensively about music.

In this period Italian opera attained a Romantic dramatic style based on novelistic librettos and lyric vocal expression. Vincenzo Bellini and Gaetano Donizetti pioneered the new style, and it reached its culmination in the first period of Giuseppe Verdi's work. In France the grand opera responded to the public taste for the striking and spectacular. The genre was developed most notably by the librettist Eugène Scribe and the composer Giacomo Meyerbeer.

The virtuoso performer became a cult figure, though some of the virtuoso solo music of the time consisted of empty showpieces. Among the great virtuosos of the concert stage were the violinist Nicolo Paganini and the pianist Franz Liszt. Frederic Chopin combined pianistic virtuosity with the lyricism of Italian operatic singing style in works generally intended for the salon rather than the public hall.

The song and piano character piece filled the needs of the salon and drawing room of the Romantic period. These intimate genres were cultivated by such first-rank composers as Felix Mendelssohn and Robert Schumann.

In the field of orchestral music the symphony still thrived, but other genres explored the possibilities of program music, notably works of Mendelssohn and Hector Berlioz. Among these were the concert overture and the program symphony. Combinations of vocal forces with the orchestra also appeared.

New traits of style grew up in the mature phase of Romanticism. Both the timbral and harmonic vocabulary expanded. Forms became freer of conventional procedures, and composers consequently called on literary archetypes or programs to clarify their unusual musical structures. Organic integration of form in cyclic structures became a Romantic characteristic.

OBJECTIVES

1. To acquaint the student with the lives and activities of Romantic composers.

2. To familiarize the student with the style developments of Romantic opera in Italy and France in the second quarter of the nineteenth century.

3. To introduce the student to the new genres of music in the Romantic period.

4. To help the student understand the characteristics of Romantic musical style.

TERMS, NAMES, AND CONCEPTS

Felix Mendelssohn Bartholdy
Franz Liszt
Frédéric Chopin
Hector Berlioz
Giuseppe Verdi
Traité d'instrumentation
Robert Schumann
Neue Zeitschrift für Musik
Davidsbund
Clara Wieck
Gaetano Donizetti
Vincenzo Bellini
scena ed aria
cavatina
cabaletta
bel canto
grand opera
Eugène Scribe
Giacomo Meyerbeer
Nicolò Paganini
Franz Hünten
Henri Herz
mazurka
polonaise
Stephen Collins Foster
Fanny Mendelssohn Hensel
character piece
    Bagatelle
    Impromptu
    Moment musical
    Nocturne
    Lied ohne Worte
concert overture

program symphony
idée fixe
plot archetype
cyclicism
Singakademie
Bach-Gesellschaft

CLASSROOM APPROACHES, ASSIGNMENTS, TOPICS FOR DISCUSSION

Writings of Romantic Composers

Read with the class some excerpts from Schumann's writings, such as the review of Chopin's op. 2 included in Oliver Strunk, ed., *Source Readings in Music History*. Discuss his writing as literature and as analysis. Have students listen to Schumann's *Carnaval* and write an essay on that music in the style of Schumann's review.

Opera

Have students watch a film or videotape of a Verdi opera in class. Discuss the Romantic characteristics of the opera. How does the subject matter reflect Romantic interests? How is it connected to the composer's own life experience? What aspects of the music differ from Classic expectations and style? How is the visual element of the production Romantic?

Music in the Salon and Drawing Room

Have students re-create a nineteenth-century salon. They should choose topics for conversation from nineteenth-century politics or art. Students may wish to read some poetry aloud, sketch portraits or caricatures. They should perform music such as songs and piano character pieces or other chamber music. Compositions by some of the fine women composers of the time should be included. (Refreshments might be served.)

Romantic Musical Style

Have students listen in class to one of the orchestral works of Berlioz. Pick out some passages in which particular instruments are featured and read what the composer had to say about the expressive use of those instruments in his *Traité d'instrumentation*.

Play for students a Romantic orchestral piece or movement (either explicitly programmatic or not). Have them write a program or adapt a familiar story to go with the music. Their writing should reflect both the character of the music and the form of the piece. Discuss the value and limitations of drawing on literary models to help in the understanding of music.

MUSIC FOR STUDY

Felix Mendelssohn Bartholdy (1809–1847), Overture to **A Midsummer Night's Dream**

Style features

The instrumentation is highly typical of Mendelssohn. Themes are used to characterize the dramatis personae—the opening chords for Oberon and his magic, the principal theme for Puck and the fairies, the transitional material for Theseus and his court at the hunt, the secondary theme for the sweethearts, the closing material for the rustic clowns. The functions of these ideas may be verified in the incidental music for the play, written many years later. The form is a rather clear sonata form and does not attempt to follow the course of the action in the play.

Score

NS 2, 96–149

SSHS 2, 152–180

Hector Berlioz (1803–1869), **Symphonie fantastique**

Style features

The *Symphonie fantastique* is probably the best-known example of the adaptation of the sonata-plan symphony to a programmatic sequence of events. The work is unified by the cyclical appearance of the idée fixe theme in all five movements. The use of the "Dies irae" melody in the fifth movement exemplifies a composer's use of material that requires a certain degree of musical literacy from the listener.

Berlioz's imaginative and innovative instrumentation is evident in all the movements, but probably most obviously in the last two.

Scores

AMSS, 256–294—third and fourth movements

* NS 2, 42–95—fifth movement

SSHS 2, 180–190—third movement

The score and accompanying historical and analytic essays are available in the edition by Edward T. Cone in the Norton Critical Scores series (New York, 1971).

Robert Schumann (1810–1856), **Carnaval**

Style features

Schumann's piano style is well illustrated in this work (except in "Chopin"). The individual pieces are based on dance rhythms and forms. A wide variety of characters are portrayed, including Schumann's alter egos Florestan and Eusebius, Clara Wieck, Chopin, and Paganini. The whole is held together by the cyclical occurrences of the motives notated at the center of the score as "Sphinxes."

Score

AMSS, 314–318—"Pierrot," "Arlequin," and "Valse noble"

Fanny Mendelssohn Hensel (1805–1847), "Schwanenlied"

Style features

The scoring of the piano part is designed to establish the general atmosphere of the poem without attempting word-painting, and it is entirely subordinate to the vocal line. The song represents the strophic type of Lied following the tradition of the Second Berlin School.

Score

HAMW, 113–118

Frederic Chopin (1810–1849), Nocturne in E-flat Major, op. 9, no. 2 (1830–1831)

Style features

The piano style is characteristic of Chopin, with a left-hand accompaniment figuration spread over a wide range in the lower and middle portions of the piano keyboard. The melody shows the influence of the Italian Romantic bel canto opera in its changing florid ornamentations of the main idea. The harmony illustrates the principle of the chromatic overloading of the conventional symmetrical phrase structure.

Score

* NAWM 2, 236-234

Clara Wieck Schumann (1819–1896), Trio in G Minor for Violin, Cello, and Piano, op. 17 (1846), first movement

Style features

This Trio represents the continuing Classic traditions in the nineteenth century and the application of Romantic melodic and harmonic style within Classic sonata-plan models. The work demonstrates not only the composer's style on her own instrument, the piano, but also her mastery of writing for the string instruments and of the problems of composing for chamber ensembles. The movement is in a clear sonata form.

Score

HAMW, 119–129

Franz Lizst (1811–1886), **Années de pèlerinage,** *2ème annèe, Italie: 5. Sonnetto 104 del Petrarca*

Style features

Liszt's interpretation of Petrarch's sonnet 104 demonstrates his typical pianistic scorings. After an introduction comes a passage that employs melody in each hand with a recitativelike accompaniment of short chords. There follow several singing melodic sections over different types of rolling left-hand accompaniment. These are framed by free, improvisatory transitions.

Score

* NS 2, 224–228

Giuseppe Verdi (1813–1901), **Il trovatore,** *Part 4, scene 1*

Style features

This is a large bipartite *scena* for Leonora, incorporating recitative dialogue at the beginning, a slow and sad love song in a minor key, an interlude with offstage chorus and the voice of the condemned troubadour, and a fast major-key aria in two sections.

Scores

* NAWM 2, 518–534—concludes before the final aria passage

SSHS 2, 275–288

SAMPLE TEST QUESTIONS

Multiple Choice

1. The composer _____ worked as a music critic and founded the *Neue Zeitschrift für Musik,* an independent music journal.

   A. Frédéric Chopin
   B. Franz Liszt
   C. Felix Mendelssohn
   D. Robert Schumann
   E. Clara Wieck Schumann

2. The Italian composers of the Romantic period developed a structure for the large solo operatic number in_____large parts.

   A. 2
   B. 3
   C. 4
   D. 5
   E. 6

3. The "dissimilar duet" was designed to express dramatic conflict in opera by the composer _____.

   A. Vincenzo Bellini
   B. Frédéric Chopin
   C. Gaetano Donizetti
   D. Giacomo Meyerbeer
   E. Giuseppe Verdi

4. Eugène Scribe made his important contributions to the history of music as a _____.

   A. composer of French grand opera
   B. librettist
   C. music teacher
   D. virtuoso performer
   E. music historian

5. Nicolò Paganini made his important contributions to the history of music as a _____.

   A. composer of French grand opera
   B. librettist
   C. music teacher
   D. virtuoso performer
   E   music historian

6. The mazurka was a type of _____ for piano based on a
    Polish dance and used by Chopin.

    A. program symphony
    B. ballad
    C. character piece
    D. nocturne
    E. song without words

7. Berlioz's *Symphonie fantastique* is an example of the genre
    _____.

    A. character piece
    B. concert overture
    C. dramatic symphony
    D. idée fixe
    E. program symphony

8. The composer_____ was one of the most imaginative
    orchestrators of the Romantic period and even wrote a treatise on
    the subject.

    A. Vincenzo Bellini
    B. Hector Berlioz
    C. Franz Liszt
    D. Felix Mendelssohn
    E. Robert Schumann

9. _____ stands as an abstract symbol in music of the
    Romantic thinker's search for the unity in all things.

    A. Bel canto
    B. Cyclic unification
    C. Harmonic overloading
    D. Risorgimento
    E. Virtuosity

10. The conductor_____ has an important place in music
    history for his role in reviving the works of preceding generations
    in his performances.

    A. Franz Liszt
    B. Felix Mendelssohn
    C. Nicolò Paganini
    D. Eugène Scribe
    E. Robert Schumann

True-False/Justification

1. Few Romantic composers made their whole living as composers.

2. The *Davidsbund* was a group of musicians and music lovers who met to discuss music.

3. The Italian Romantic opera composers continued to concentrate on mythological stories in their works.

4. Verdi's operas often reflect concerns in his own life experience.

5. French opera audiences in the nineteenth century, like their Baroque predecessors, enjoyed stage spectacle and grandeur.

6. The cult of virtuosity in the nineteenth century was a manifestation of a romantic tendency.

7. Conditions in the nineteenth century were such that although women could be poets or novelists they could not become composers.

8. The concert overture was an orchestral piece that took its form from a literary structure rather than musical convention.

9. *Carnaval*, Schumann's Fourth Symphony, and *Harold en Italie* all employ literary material to unify their structures.

10. The first scholarly edition of a historical composer's works began to be issued in the middle of the nineteenth century.

Short Essay

Explain several different ways in which the lives of Romantic composers affect their compositions.

How were the conventions of Classic musical structure suited to adaptation to the characteristic and programmatic musical styles of Romanticism?

ANSWERS TO SAMPLE TEST QUESTIONS

Multiple Choice

1. D   Robert Schumann
2. A   2
3. C   Gaetano Donizetti
4. B   librettist
5. D   virtuoso performer
6. C   character piece
7. E   program symphony

8. B Hector Berlioz
9. B Cyclic unification
10. B Felix Mendelssohn

True-False/Justification

1. T Many Romantic composers worked as performers, teachers, or writers.

2. T Robert Schumann used the conversations of the members of his fictional *Davidsbund* as a medium for his music criticism.

3. F Italian Romantic operas turned toward novelistic subjects and contemporary writers.

4. T Verdi often dealt with stories of difficult family relationships and political conflict, both subjects that figure prominently in his biography.

5. T The grand opera responded to the French audience's love of the spectacular in opera.

6. T The virtuoso's role as artistic hero or priest of a mystical experience arose from a romantic view of music.

7. F Although nineteenth-century social structures did not foster women composers, such women as Fanny Mendelssohn Hensel and Clara Wieck Schumann did compose fine music.

8. F The concert overture is more characteristic than programmatic and usually employs conventional processes such as sonata form.

9. F Unity is provided by recurring thematic material in *Carnaval*, Schumann's Fourth Symphony, and *Harold en Italie*.

10. T Publication of the Bach-Gesellschaft edition of J. S. Bach's music began in 1850.

CHAPTER 21

THE TWILIGHT OF ROMANTICISM

CHAPTER OVERVIEW

Progressive thinking in music after 1850 was led by the New German School composers, Liszt and Richard Wagner. They argued for freedom from the constraints of Classic conventions of form, placing emphasis on the emotional content of music. In conjunction with this, they linked music to other art forms even more closely than their Romantic predecessors had done. Liszt invented a new program-music genre, the symphonic poem, and Wagner brought the arts together in the music drama, a Gesamtkunstwerk. Both took as their stylistic models the symphonic development with its freedom of structure and unifying exploration of musical motives.

In opposition to the New German style some composers continued to work essentially within the tradition of Romanticism, finding new personal expressions without radical changes in the style they inherited. Among these late Romantic composers were Johannes Brahms in Vienna, composers in France, and Italian opera composers.

Some of the most advanced opera composers in the late-nineteenth-century took up the literature of the realist movement as the model for their librettos. This is well illustrated by the verismo operas of Italy. The musical style that supported operatic realism challenged the voices of the singers and extended the Romantic orchestration and harmony to express uncontrolled and violent passion.

Dissatisfaction with the existing styles of Western music led composers to turn to other cultures for musical ideas, producing the movement known as exoticism. It became typical of composers from the peripheral regions of Europe to seek to free themselves from the stylistic domination of the main tradition. This was partly because the old ideas seemed effete and partly an expression of the political nationalism that was rising at the time. The nationalist composers introduced rhythms and forms based on those of national dances and the modal melodies of folk tunes into concert and operatic genres.

OBJECTIVES

1. To help the student understand the principles and style of the New German School.

2. To familiarize the student with the music of the late Romantic period.

3. To acquaint the student with realism in late-nineteenth-century opera.

4. To give the student an understanding of the causes and styles of exoticism and nationalism in the music of the late nineteenth century.

TERMS, NAMES, AND CONCEPTS

New German School
"the music of the future"
symphonic poem
thematic transformation
Richard Wagner
Das Kunstwerk der Zukunft
Gesamtkunstwerk
music drama
    Der Ring des Nibelunaen
    Tristan und Isolde
    Die Meistersinger von Nürnberg
    Parsifal
Stabreim
"Wagner tuba"
unendliche Melodie
Leitmotiv
late Romanticism
Eduard Hanslick
Johannes Brahms
Anton Bruckner
lyric opera
Charles Gounod
mélodie
César Franck
Arrigo Boito
post-Romantic
Hugo Wolf
Gustav Mahler
Richard Strauss
tone poem
Alexander Scriabin
mystic chord
realism
Georges Bizet
verismo
Pietro Mascagni
Ruggero Leoncavallo
Giacomo Puccini

exoticism
Félicien David
Louis Moreau Gottschalk
Sebastian Iradier
Universal Exhibition of 1889
nationalism
Bedřich Smetana
Antonin Dvořák
Mikhail Glinka
Alexander Dargomyzhsky
Pyotr Il'yich Tchaikovsky
moguchay kuchka (mighty five)
Alexander Borodin
Cesar Cui
Mily Balakirev
Modest Mussorgsky
Nicolai Rimsky-Korsakov
Edvard Grieg
Isaac Albéniz
Edward Elgar
Edward MacDowell
Second New England School
John Knowles Paine
George Whitefield Chadwick
Horatio Parker
Amy Beach

CLASSROOM APPROACHES, ASSIGNMENTS, TOPICS FOR DISCUSSION

New German School

The phrase "music of the future" may be used to recall to students some earlier slogans or titles for music that was heralded as groundbreaking. Have students identify the similarities and differences among the periods of the "ars nova," *Le nuove musiche,* and "the music of the future." What was the nature of the revolutionary idea in each case? How significant was the change in musical principles each represents?

Students should see rather than merely hear at least a substantial portion of one of Wagner's music dramas. In class discussion have them consider how important the visual and gestural elements are to the understanding of the Gesamtkunstwerk. Films or videotapes are available, including some of the more experimental stagings, and the latter may be used to raise questions about (1) the flexibility of great works to be adapted to new situations and (2) problems of integrity of style in staging. Students should also confront the philosophical issues in Wagner's works. The *Ring* dramas and *Tristan und Isolde* are frequently anthologized and explore broad and profound questions. *Die Meistersinger* provides an opportunity to discuss the principle of the "music of the future," since it deals explicitly with the artist's freedom from conventional limits.

Discuss with students the advantages and disadvantages of an opera composer's writing his own libretto. Do the works and the aesthetic theories of Wagner now force composers to justify *not* creating their own opera librettos?

For written or oral in-class reports students may be assigned to write on the relationships between Wagner and some important nineteenth-century philosophers: Hegel's idea of the development of history and its influence on the idea of artistic progress for the New German School; Schopenhauer's conception of the Will and its relationship to *Tristan und Isolde*; social and economic criticism in the writings of Karl Marx and in *Der Ring des Nibelungen*.

Discuss with students the place of post-Romanticism in relation to the development of the Classic-Romantic style. Would it be justifiable to regard post-Romanticism as a mannerist phase? Does the music drama represent a logical extension of the dramatic expressive basis of all music in the Classic-Romantic period?

Late Romanticism and Post-Romanticism

Assign students make a chart under the headings "Late Romantic" and "Post-Romantic." In each category they should list (1) prominent composers, (2) style characteristics, (3) typical genres. They should notice that chamber ensemble music and piano music belong more to late Romanticism; program music belongs more to post-Romanticism; and symphony, song, and opera appear in both categories. They should also be able to explain these cases.

Exoticism and Nationalism

This is a good time to expand students' awareness of other music cultures. Play in class some recorded examples of music of other cultures and of compositions based on those styles—Middle Eastern music and Félicien David's *Le Désert*; Spanish music and Bizet's exoticism; Japanese music and excerpts from *Madama Butterfly*; and eastern European folk music and nineteenth-century nationalist works. Students should identify what aspects of the non-Western musical styles are incorporated into exoticist or nationalist compositions, and what elements of those compositions belong to the Western tradition.

Ask students to consider the artistic problems for a nationalist composer in the use of folk melodies in sonata-form structures. Why might a folk tune not fulfill the tonal function expected from the themes in sonata form? If the form were constructed on the basis of a thematic rather than tonal foundation, what might happen to the conventional tonal plan?

MUSIC FOR STUDY

Richard Wagner (1813–1883), **Die Walküre,** *Act 3, scene 3*

Style features

This excerpt may be used to illustrate all the characteristic features of Wagner's style in the music dramas: the expanded orchestra, use of motives, extended harmonic planning combined with free modulation, dramatic developing form, and the literary style of the libretto.

Scores

ARM, 334–367—piano-vocal score

SSHS 2, 289–300—Wotan's farewell only, piano-vocal score

Johannes Brahms (1833–1897), **Ein deutsches Requiem,** *op. 45, "Wie lieblich sind deine Wohnungen"*

Style features

The "conservative" elements of the work include the scoring for an orchestra of no more than late Classic size, the structural clarity, and the "academic" counterpoint of the double fugue (meas. 124ff). Romanticism is evident in the expression of the text, in the lyric melodic line introduced by the tenors (meas. 25ff), and in the general richness of scoring and harmony.

Score

SSHS 2, 300-311

Georges Bizet (1838-1875), **Carmen,** *Act 1, "Habañera"*

Style features

The scoring, rhythm, and harmony produce a stylized evocation of the flamenco style of Spanish music. The melody of this song was actually the work of Sebastian Iradier, though Bizet understood it to be a Spanish folk tune. The piece is strophic in two stanzas.

Score

MRP, 762–773

Modest Mussorgsky (1839–1881), **Boris Godunov,** *Act 3, Boris's monologue*

Style features

The general tone of the monologue captures the introspective, brooding spirit of Russian Romanticism. The scorings of Mussorgsky and Rimsky-Korsakov are both available in current recordings and should be compared. Boris's vocal line shows the style of naturalistic declamation Mussorgsky employed in place of Western operatic style. The structure of the scene is free.

Score

MRP, 831–839

Franz Liszt, "Nuages gris" (1881)

Style features

In this brief and extremely concentrated example, technical pianism and most of the elements of style are subordinated to experimentation with unconventional harmony. The augmented triad dominates, and harmonic motion is nonfunctional.

Score

 * NAWM 2, 254–255

Antonin Dvořák (1841–1904), Piano Quintet in A major, op. 81, second movement, "Dumka"

Style features

This movement demonstrates the combination of nationalistic material with a standard Classic-Romantic genre and form of chamber music. The piece adopts a rondo form. The rondo theme is modeled on the style of the Ukrainian-Bohemian dumka, a lamenting folk song.

Score

MRP, 794–816

Amy Beach (1867–1944), Symphony in E minor "Gaelic," first movement

Style features

The general style of the symphony is that of late Romanticism. The movement employs sonata form, but with nearly continuous use of motivic-developmental style. The influence of exoticism is evident in Beach's use of a melody in a Gaelic idiom.

Source

HAMW, 166–203

Gustav Mahler (1860–1911), Kindertotenlieder, *"Nun will die Sonn' so hell aufgeh'n"*

Style features

Mahler's colorful and transparent style of scoring is well illustrated by this example. The characteristically thorough dynamic and interpretive markings should be noted (including repeated exhortations to be expressive). The harmony is post-Romantic.

Scores

AAM, 653-659

* NAWM 2, 352-363

SAMPLE TEST QUESTIONS

Multiple Choice

1. The progressive composers working in Germany in the period after 1850 became known as the _____.

    A. Davidsbund
    B. Ring of the Nibelung
    C. realists
    D. Volk
    E. New German School

2. In his symphonic poems, Lizst employed _____ to develop structural coherence in unconventional forms.

    A. Gesamtkunstwerk
    B. idées fixes
    C. thematic transformation
    D. Leitmotivs
    E. Grundthemen

3. Wagner's *Tristan und Isolde* is an example of the genre he called
    _____.

    A. music drama
    B. lyric opera
    C. tone poem
    D. *Der Ring des Nibelungen*
    E. concert overture

4. A musical idea in Wagner's mature works, often associated with an
    idea or character in the plot and developed in symphonic style in
    the orchestra, is usually called a _____, a term the
    composer himself did not use.

    A. thematic transformation
    B. moguchay kuchka
    C. Stabreim
    D. Leitmotiv
    E. verismo

5. The composer _____ took up the tradition of Mendelssohn
    and Schumann and later provided important support to the career
    of Dvořák.

    A. Brahms
    B. Franck
    C. Liszt
    D. Mussorgsky
    E. Wagner

6. Verdi's last two operas were both adapted from works of
    _____, who was an important figure to nineteenth-century
    literary thought.

    A. Lord Byron
    B. Alexandre Dumas
    C. Johann Wolfgang von Goethe
    D. Friedrich Schiller
    E. William Shakespeare

7. The post-Romantic composer Gustav Mahler based several of his
    symphonies on material taken from _____.

    A. his own Lieder
    B. Lutheran chorales
    C. Wagner's music
    D. exotic melodies
    E. American folk songs

8. The_____ employed plots that featured violent emotional outbreaks in characters from the lower classes and a musical style based on declamatory singing and powerful orchestration.

   A. lyric opera
   B. music drama
   C. grand opera
   D. verismo opera
   E. Second New England School

9. Composers seeking to revitalize the European musical tradition in the late nineteenth century turned to _____, the use of materials derived from musical styles from outside the leading nations of Europe.

   A. the music of the future
   B. verismo
   C. Volk
   D. exoticism
   E. nationalism

10. The_____ was an important group of nationalist composers in the late nineteenth century.

   A. Second Berlin School
   B. New German School
   C. Second New England School
   D. Second Vienna School
   E. moguchay kuchka

True-False/Justification

1. Liszt followed the model of Berlioz in composing program symphonies.

2. The term *unendliche Melodie* refers to the extremely long and florid vocal phrases in Wagner's style.

3. Eduard Hanslick was one of the leading composers who followed in the footsteps of Wagner.

4. The nineteenth-century *chanson* was the equivalent of the German Lied in the history of the art song.

5. The genre of lyric opera was created in France as a reaction to the bombast of grand opera.

6. The art song died out in German-speaking countries after the middle of the nineteenth century.

7. The works of Bedřich Smetana and Antonin Dvořák represent the nationalist movement in Hungary, which in the late nineteenth century attempted to throw off Austrian domination.

8. The leader of the Mighty Five was the composer Boris Godunov, who was the only one who had a formal conservatory training.

9. Promising American composers of the late nineteenth century usually traveled abroad for their musical education.

10. The United States produced no important woman composer until after the middle of the twentieth century.

Short Essay

Discuss in what ways the "music of the future" movement in the late nineteenth century rejected the musical assumptions established in the Classic phase of musical style, and in what ways it remained based on those assumptions.

Both Russian and American composers in the late nineteenth century found themselves geographically at the periphery of the mainstream European cultural tradition. How and why did their approaches to musical style differ?

ANSWERS TO SAMPLE TEST QUESTIONS

Multiple Choice

1. E   New German School
2. C   thematic transformation
3. A   music drama
4. D   Leitmotiv
5. A   Brahms
6. E   William Shakespeare
7. A   his own Lieder
8. D   verismo opera
9. D   exoticism
10. E   moguchay kuchka

True-False/Justification

1. T   Liszt's *Dante* Symphony and *Faust* Symphony are program symphonies .

2. F   *Unendliche Melodie* refers to musical structure which is not built in conventional four-square period structure and does not include passages of nonthematic "filler" material.

3. F   Hanslick was a writer who opposed the New German School.

4. F   The French art song was called *mélodie; chanson* was the term used for a folk song or popular song.

5. T   Lyric opera met the need for interpretation of more intimate and personal subjects.

6. F   Important art songs were composed by Brahms and the post-Romantic composers Hugo Wolf and Gustav Mahler.

7. F   Smetana and Dvořák were Bohemian composers.

8. F   Boris Godunov was the Czar of Russia in around 1600 and the subject of an opera by Mussorgsky.

9. T   A European conservatory education was still considered desirable for serious composers in the late Romantic period.

10. F   Amy Beach (1867–1944) became a significant composer.

CHAPTER 22

THE ARRIVAL OF THE TWENTIETH CENTURY

CHAPTER OVERVIEW

The radical changes in musical style in the second half of the nineteenth century called into question basic assumptions about musical aesthetics and style. Around the turn of the century several new approaches appeared in response to this crisis.

Impressionism in music, paralleling the impressionist and symbolist movements in literature and painting, proposed that music should arise principally from sensual criteria. The leading composer of this style was Claude Debussy. The music of the movement stressed the elements of music that are perceived most immediately—timbre and harmonic color—placing less emphasis on those elements that unfold over time, such as rhythm and melody, and subordinating structure.

Other composers extended the expressive intensity of post-Romanticism and of realism, challenging the assumption that music should necessarily seek to be beautiful. Primitivism followed exoticism in deriving inspiration from other cultures, and it stressed percussive timbres, dissonant harmony, irregular rhythm, and improvisatory melodic patterns. The expressionist composers took up the chromatic harmonic language of post-Romanticism and increased dissonance until they achieved atonality, conveying the effect of psychotic emotional instability.

In the United States Charles Ives worked in new and personal directions, inspired by the ideals of free thinking espoused by the New England transcendentalist philosophers. The most distinctively American composer up to his time, he led the way for his successors into avant-garde compositional style.

OBJECTIVES

1. To help the student understand the aesthetic principles of impressionism and their effect on musical style.

2. To give the student an understanding of the thinking that led to primitivism and expressionism in the arts and the stylistic consequences of that thinking for music.

3. To acquaint the student with the ideas and music of Charles Ives.

TERMS, NAMES AND CONCEPTS

impressionism
symbolism
Claude Debussy
  Prélude à l'après-midi d'un faune
  La Mer
  Pelléas et Mélisande
chord "streaming"
whole-tone scale
pentatonic scale
primitivism
Béla Bartók
Igor Stravinsky
  Le sacre du printemps
Serge Diaghilev
Vaclav Nijinsky
polychords
expressionism
stream of consciousness
Second Vienna School
Arnold Schoenberg
  Pierrot lunaire
atonality
Sprechstimme
Alban Berg
  Wozzeck
Charles Ives
  Concord Sonata
avant-garde
polymeter
microtones, quarter tones
cluster chords
collage technique

CLASSROOM APPROACHES, ASSIGNMENTS, TOPICS FOR DISCUSSION

Impressionism

Hold a debate in class on the proposition "RESOLVED: that Claude Debussy's music should be regarded as symbolist rather than impressionist."

Primitivism

Assign half the class to listen to several examples of non-Western music of oral and tribal cultures, such as the folk music of Africans and

Native Americans, and to make as detailed a list of their style characteristics as they can. Assign the other half of the class to do the same for some examples of primitivism in Western music of the period around 1910. Compare the lists of style traits. Ask students to identify what aspects of primitivist music resemble those of the tribal music cultures and what aspects belong to the Western musical tradition.

Expressionism

Discuss in class the validity of expressionism as a cultural expression of Western life in the last decade of the twentieth century. Do students feel that expressionist art reflects their own personal condition? the social situation in the United States? Can students identify expressionism in examples of contemporary popular music?

Discuss with students the way in which dissonance and atonality create musical tension. Do they believe that the instability expressed by dissonance is absolute, or that it is relative and depends on contrast with consonance? In the latter case, does atonality soon undermine its own effect of intensity because there is no point of stability to give the instability of atonality meaning?

Charles Ives

Have students reflect on what makes a composer "Americanistic." Can they identify style traits that were common to leading American composers from the time of the Revolution to World War I? Have there been characteristically American aesthetic ideals? How nationalistic were each of the following: Francis Hopkinson, William Billings, James Hewitt, Stephen Foster, Edward MacDowell, composers of the Second New England School, Charles Ives?

MUSIC FOR STUDY

Claude Debussy (1862–1918), Nocturnes, "Nuages"

Style features

Debussy's impressionistic style of scoring here includes the use of muted and multiply-divided strings and the quasi-oriental sound of unison flute and harp. The rhythm is ambiguous particularly at the beginning, where the signature is $\frac{6}{8}$ but the pattern produces a grouping that suggests $\frac{3}{4}$. Melody is often reduced to mere fragments, as in the English horn phrase (meas. 5–8) or the horn motive (meas. 22–23). Impressionistic harmonic language is evident in the nonfunctional streams of parallel chords (meas. 14 etc.) and the pentatonic melody of the middle section (meas. 64–79—all on "black-key" notes). The form is ternary, but the return of the opening is abbreviated, very fragmentary in its texture, and incorporates a reference to the middle part.

Score

* NAWM 2, 540–556

Arnold Schoenberg (1874–1951), **Pierrot lunaire,** *excerpts*

Style features

Expressionist style is evident here first of all in the atonality of the work. The scoring is for chamber ensemble and vocalist, using Sprechstimme throughout. The tightly knit texture, using contrapuntal and motivic-developmental techniques, compensates for the lack of tonal coherence.

Scores

AAM, 754–761

AMSS, 422–427—Nos. 1, 8

* NAWM 2, 646–653—Nos. 8, 13

Igor Stravinsky (1882–1971), **Le sacre du printemps,** *excerpts*

Style features

Primitivism is evident in the uncontrolled rhythms and empirical polyphonic textures of the introduction. The Danses des adolescentes and Rondes de printemps illustrate the use of heavily accented percussive rhythms with changing beat groupings, simple melodic cells, and polychords.

Scores

AAM, 700–716—Introduction, Rondes de printemps

AMSS, 444–461—Danses des adolescentes

* NAWM 2, 590–608—Danses des adolescentes

SSHS 2, 383–397—Introduction, Les augures printaniers (Danses des adolescentes)

Lili Boulanger (1893–1918), **Clairières dans le ciel,** *"Demain fera un an"*

Style features

The song shows the characteristics of impressionism. The piano scoring is interesting and varied, employing all registers of the instrument and several different figurations. The vocal style tends to be rhythmically free and declamatory. The expressive markings are evocative and characteristic of the style. The general intent is to establish moods of the symbolist text, which is by Francis Jammes.

The form of the song is rondolike; it also connects cyclically to the other songs of the cycle.

Score

HAMW, 232–244

Alban Berg (1885–1935), Wozzeck, Act 3

Style features

Wozzeck makes a very convincing example of expressionism in its content and style. The opera employs a large orchestra, sometimes used lightly in chamberlike ensembles. The vocal techniques called for include singing, speech, and Sprechstimme. The music is frequently atonal, though there are passages that illustrate tonality (the interlude on B after scene 2) and bitonality (scene 3). Form is tightly controlled by the organization of the act into five scenes and an interlude, each constituting an invention on a different type of musical idea: theme, tone, rhythm, chord, key.

Scores

* NAWM 2, 722–739—Act 3, scene 3

* NS 2, 934–958—Act 3, scenes 4–5

SSHS 2, 398–409—Act III, scenes 1–2

Charles Ives (1874–1954), "Charlie Rutlage"

Style features

The vocalist in this song not only sings but also speaks using specified rhythms. The piano part includes cluster chords to be played by fists, as well as a variety of figurations that suggest different musical genres. The accompanist's part incorporates a phrase from a cowboy song, "Whoopee ti yi yo, git along little dogies." Despite the free chromaticism and dissonance of much of the song, melodic pentatonicism gives it a folklike effect.

Scores

MTC, 70–74

SSHS 2, 418–422

SAMPLE TEST QUESTIONS

Multiple Choice

1. The nationality most closely associated with the impressionist movement was _____.

    A. Austria
    B. England
    C. France
    D. Russia
    E. the United States

2. The most important element of style in impressionist music is _____.

    A. scoring
    B. rhythm
    C. melody
    D. texture
    E. form

3. The _____ scale provides no feeling of tonal directedness because all its intervals are equal in size.

    A. major
    B. minor
    C. pentatonic
    D. phrygian
    E. whole-tone

4. Percussive timbres, pounding irregular rhythms, and dissonant harmonies are characteristic of _____ music.

    A. expressionist
    B. impressionist
    C. primitivist
    D. Russian
    E. Viennese

5. Stream of consciousness is to literary expressionism as _____ is (are) to expressionism in music.

    A. atonality
    B. pentatonicism
    C. chord streaming
    D. quarter tones
    E. antiphonal ensembles

6. The leader of _____ was Arnold Schoenberg.

    A. the Second New England School
    B. the Second Berlin School
    C. the Second Vienna School
    D. les fauves
    E. the transcendentalist philosophers

7. The vocal style in which the performer uses the timbre of regular speech but follows a contour of high and low pitch is called _____.

    A. primitivism
    B. "Art poétique"
    C. stream of consciousness
    D. microtones
    E. Sprechstimme

8. The aesthetic viewpoint of Charles Ives was most strongly influenced by the thinking of _____.

    A. Wagner
    B. Dostoevsky
    C. Freud
    D. Emerson
    E. Buchner

9. Ives's Second Piano Sonata is named for the city of _____.

    A. Berlin
    B. Concord
    C. Paris
    D. Vienna
    E. none of the above

10. _____ pioneered in the use of collage technique in musical composition.

    A. Béla Bartók
    B. Alban Berg
    C. Claude Debussy
    D. Charles Ives
    E. Arnold Schoenberg

True-False/Justification

1. The term *impressionism* was borrowed for music from painting.

2. The aesthetic basis for impressionism in music was a new acoustical theory invented by physicists working with new technologies developed at the beginning of the twentieth century.

3. The harmonies in impressionist music move in nonfunctional successions because this resembles the use of stream-of-consciousness technique in symbolist poetry.

4. The roots of expressionism were in late-nineteenth-century literary realism.

5. Stravinsky's ballet *L'oiseau de feu* caused a crisis because its primitivism shocked the Parisian audience at its premiere performance.

6. Arnold Schoenberg was an expressionist artist not only as a composer.

7. Schoenberg's *Pierrot lunaire* follows in the tradition of the song cycle.

8. Alban Berg's *Wozzeck* adopts Classic musical forms to organize its musical structure.

9. Charles Ives made a tremendous impression on the musical world and on the development of styles when he composed his works in the period just before the First World War.

10. Ives was not only a composer but also a writer.

Short Essay

How did impressionism and expressionism each respond to Wagnerism?

What were the ideas of Debussy, Schoenberg, and Ives about the place of beauty in music?

ANSWERS TO SAMPLE TEST QUESTIONS

Multiple Choice

1. C   France
2. A   scoring
3. E   whole-tone
4. C   primitivist
5. A   atonality

6. C   the Second Vienna School
7. E   Sprechstimme
8. D   Emerson
9. B   Concord
10. D   Charles Ives

True-False/Justification

1. T   The word *impressionism* first appeared in a review of a painting by Claude Monet.

2. F   Impressionism is based on sensual appeal in music.

3. F   Nonfunctional harmony in impressionist music helps to avoid the suggestion of emotional tension.

4. T   Realism anticipated the powerful and uncontrolled emotions expressed in expressionism.

5. F   The ballet that caused a scandal because of its primitivist style was *Le sacre du printemps*.

6. T   Schoenberg also painted in an expressionist style.

7. T   *Pierrot lunaire* resembles the nineteenth-century song cycle in employing a coherent set of texts unified by a single topic and by a single poet, though it is scored for Sprechstimme and chamber ensemble.

8. T   *Wozzeck* incorporates a suite, a symphony, and a series of inventions.

9. F   Ives's works were largely ignored for a number of years after they were composed.

10. T   Ives's writings deal with both aesthetics and political issues.

CHAPTER 23

BETWEEN THE WORLD WARS

CHAPTER OVERVIEW

The decades of the 1920s and 1930s were characterized by attempts to reestablish stability and control in music and other arts as in the political and economic spheres. The twelve-tone method, developed by Schoenberg, effected this control for atonal music. Anton Webern extended the method to other elements of musical style.

In tonal music, composers sought objectivity in returns to some of the genres and structuring principles of earlier periods of music history. This produced various manifestations of neoclassicism. New sources of tonal materials appeared in original theories of tonality and in the discovery of the patterns employed in folk musics.

The influence of the need to reach a general public audience brought about conservative neo-Classic or neo-Romantic styles both in the Soviet Union under the theories of socialist realism and in the United States because of market forces and populism. The public's desire for innovative but not arcane music also led to the appeal and development of jazz, which not only became an art music in its own right but also influenced composers in more traditional genres.

The period between the two World Wars also produced a vigorous avant-garde movement. Avant-garde composers explored both unconventional tone materials and new ideas about musical structure.

OBJECTIVES

1. To help the student understand the principle of control and objectivity in the various styles of music between the World nars .

2. To familiarize the student with the basic techniques of the twelve-tone method of composition.

3. To give the student an understanding of the different tonal styles between 1917 and 1945.

4. To acquaint the student with some of the innovations of avant-garde music before 1945.

TERMS, NAMES, AND CONCEPTS

twelve-tone method
  row, set, series
  prime, original
  inversion
  retrograde
  retrograde inversion
Anton Webern
serialism
Klangfarbenmelodie
neoclassic
Erik Satie
les six
  Louis Durey
  Arthur Honegger
  Darius Milhaud
  Germaine Tailleferre
  Francis Poulenc
  Georges Auric
Poetics of Music
Paul Hindemith
The Craft of Musical Composition
Gebrauchsmusik
Béla Bartók
Zoltán Kodály
socialist realism
Dmitri Shostakovich
  Lady Macbeth of the District of Mzensk
Sergey Prokofiev
Aaron Copland
  Appalachian Spring
Nadia Boulanger
Martha Graham
Howard Hanson
Roger Sessions
jazz
Dixieland
big band
swing
George Gershwin
  Porgy and Bess
Ferruccio Busoni
Luigi Russolo
George Antheil
Edgard Varèse
Henry Cowell
Harry Partch
tone clusters
prepared piano

CLASSROOM APPROACHES, ASSIGNMENTS, TOPICS FOR DISCUSSION

Twelve-tone Method and Serialism

In class, have the students construct a twelve-tone row and write its retrograde, its inversion (which may be transposed), and retrograde inversion. Then assign students to compose brief pieces based on that material. To help control their compositions, the students might be advised to use no more than two forms of the row and to compose a piece in two parts (i.e, on the model of a bicinium for two instruments or a two-part invention for keyboard.) Students should perform some contrasting compositions in class. Discuss the styles of each piece and the ways in which two compositions derived from the same material differ.

Using the row material the class has devised, assign students to compose a brief piece for a small ensemble using serialized durations and instrumentation. Have students perform their music in class. Ask them to consider in what ways this kind of composition is easier or more difficult than more traditional procedures. Do they feel that they are able to express themselves in this style?

Review with students the use of serial procedures in the isorhythmic structures of fourteenth- and fifteenth-century motets and Masses. They should make the association of the color in an isorhythmic tenor with a pitch-class series and the talea with a rhythmic series. Raise the question whether the serial method of composition represents an abandonment of the literary models for musical expression that have guided Western ideas and styles since the fifteenth century and a return to mathematical models.

Neoclassicism

Hold a debate in class on the proposition, advanced by Stravinsky in *Poetics of Music*, that "music is, by its very nature, essentially powerless to *express* anything at all, whether a feeling, an attitude of mind, a psychological mood, a phenomenon of nature, etc." The students should consider what Stravinsky meant by that statement and the historical context in which he made it.

Have students review the concept of Gebrauchsmusik. They should understand that, for much of the history of Western music, functional music was the norm. When did that change, and why? How does functionalism relate to the development of musical style?

The Composer and the Public

Discuss with students the relationship between the composer and the public in the twentieth century. They should consider the following issues:

To what extent should the public's ability to comprehend music constrain the composer's creativity?

What role should government have in encouraging music and the other arts? What should be government's role in directing artistic expression for the public good? Compare the doctrine of socialist realism to Plato's theories in the *Republic*.

Compare the division between "serious" and popular music to the situation in earlier historical periods.

The Avant-garde

Review in class discussion instances of avant-garde movements in music history—i.e., ars nova, seconda prattica, "the music of the future." What causes avant-garde movements to arise? What is the usual public and critical reception of radically new styles?

MUSIC FOR STUDY

Arnold Schoenberg, Suite for Piano, op. 25, Menuett and Trio

Style features

The use of the twelve-tone method can be studied easily in this piece, Schoenberg's first complete work based on the technique. The rhythm and form are those of the Classic minuet and trio. The melodic and harmonic structure are controlled by the twelve-tone row (the matrix for which is shown in *Ideas and Styles in the Western Musical Tradition* as Figure 23.1). The Trio employs both melodic and contrapuntal inversion.

Score

ATCM, 174–177

Anton Webern (1883–1945), Concerto for Nine Instruments, op. 24, first movement

Style features

The row that serves as basis for this composition has an interesting internal organization; it is constructed out of an original three-note pattern together with transpositions of its retrograde inversion, retrograde, and inversion.

Webern applied serial procedures to the instrumentation and the rhythm in this work. Measures 63-67, for example, state the instrument series oboe, trumpet, flute, clarinet twice; at the same time the series of note values established in measures 1-3 appears in retrograde, then in original order.

Score

AAM, 790–796

Béla Bartók (1881–1945), Concerto for Orchestra, first movement

Style features

The Concerto for Orchestra recalls the Baroque genre of ripieno concerto.

The pitch organization is modal and based on fourths. The overall harmonic contrast in the movement is between areas separated by a tritone, F and B.

The movement combines sonata and Bartok's characteristic palindromic forms.

Scores

* NS 2, 830–857

SSHS 2, 356–371

Igor Stravinsky, Symphony of Psalms, *first movement*

Style features

The scoring focuses on winds and percussion; the only string instruments used are harp, piano, cello, and bass. The choral writing features unison and parallel octaves. In general, the vocal parts are chantlike or choralelike, while the orchestra presents active figurations, recalling Baroque chorale settings.

The sharp, percussive orchestral chords that interrupt the flow of the rhythm recall in a new way the Stravinskian primitivist style.

The pitch organization is tonal by assertion, based on the pervasive emphasis on E.

Scores

AAM, 717–732

* NS 2, 893–907

Aaron Copland (1900-1990), Appalachian Spring

Style features

The ballet score and the suite taken from it represent a recognizably American style. Components of this style are references to folk music, both literal, as in the variations on the Shaker song "The Gift to be Simple" and in general imitation, as in the scene of the revival preacher. In addition, American traits include the very open style of scoring and modal melodic and harmonic material.

Scores

ATCM, 64–83—excerpt from the first part of the ballet

* NAWM 2, 622–635—"The Gift to be Simple"

Ruth Crawford Seeger (1901–1953), String Quartet 1931, third movement

Style features

This highly original movement reduces rhythm and melody to a stasis that makes them quite unimportant as sources of musical interest. The dissonant harmony is coloristic rather than functional. The main source of interest is dynamics.

Score

HAMW, 285–286

Edgard Varèse (1883–1965), Ionisation

Style features

The work is scored for thirteen percussionists, mostly playing instruments of indefinite pitch. The concepts melody and harmony therefore simply do not apply to this music. The analytical vocabulary for this work has not been standardized—Varèse discussed his music in terms of the collision and interpenetration of masses and planes of sound. The rhythms are highly irregular; the meter in the score serves only to allow the players to coordinate their parts and not as an indication of perceptible rhythm patterns. Dynamics create a clear sense of shape and climax.

Score

* NS 2, 913–933

John Cage (b. 1912), Sonatas and Interludes, Nos. 1 and 5

Style features

The timbres in these pieces, produced by the prepared piano, are extremely varied. The notation is conventional in that it identifies the keys to be played, the rhythms, and pedalling; it does not relate in the conventional fashion to the indication of pitch.

Scores

AAM, 829–832

MTC, 54–56—No. 5 only

SAMPLE TEST QUESTIONS

Multiple Choice

1. The most commonly employed system for the organized composition of atonal music in the period following World War I was the twelve-tone method devised by _____.

   A. Aaron Copland
   B. Nadia Boulanger
   C. Darius Milhaud
   D. Arnold Schoenberg
   E. Anton Webern

2. When a tone row is presented upside down and backwards, we say that it appears in its _____ form.

   A. cancrizans
   B. inversion
   C. prime
   D. retrograde
   E. retrograde inversion

3. _____ extended the principle of serialization to other elements of music besides pitch organization.

   A. Béla Bartók
   B. Alban Berg
   C. Aaron Copland
   D. Paul Hindemith
   E. Anton Webern

4. Cubist painters, the Bauhaus school of architecture and design, and neoclassic composers all shared a desire to achieve _____.

   A. popular appeal
   B. objectivity
   C. emotional expression
   D. functionalism in art
   E. an avant-garde approach that would challenge the public

5. An important group of six young neoclassic composers arose in
   _____ in around 1920.

   A. England
   B. France
   C. Germany
   D. Italy
   E. the United States

6. Paul Hindemith espoused the idea of functional music or
   _____, as he called it.

   A. Gebrauchsmusik
   B. Geisslerlieder
   C. Gesamtkunstwerk
   D. Gymnopédies
   E. none of the above

7. The ideal for Soviet music in the post-revolutionary period was
   _____.

   A. avant-gardism
   B. formalism
   C. petty bourgeois
   D. socialist realism
   E. serialism

8. The American composer _____ composed several
   important ballet and film scores in the 1930s and 1940s.

   A. Nadia Boulanger
   B. John Cage
   C. Aaron Copland
   D. Martha Graham
   E. Harry Partch

9. _____ was classically trained but had his first successes
   as a popular composer and later incorporated jazz styles into major
   orchestral and operatic works.

   A. Arnold Schoenberg
   B. Béla Bartók
   C. Dmitri Shostakovich
   D. George Gershwin
   E. Harry Partch

10. Ferruccio Busoni's *Entwurf einer neuen Aesthetik der Tonkunst* (Draft for a new esthetic of music) supported the _____ movement.

    A. twelve-tone
    B. socialist realism
    C. neoclassic
    D. avant-garde
    E. jazz

True-False/Justification

1. The purpose of the twelve-tone method of composition was to support the new theory of equal temperament for the twelve tones of the chromatic scale.

2. There are 48 different possible orderings of twelve pitch classes.

3. Twelve-tone materials can be successfully combined with tonal materials in musical compositions.

4. The term Klangfarbenmelodie is used to identify music in which there is a seamless structure without cadential articulations or nonthematic "filler material."

5. Among the composers of the Second Vienna School, the one who used the idea of serialization most rigorously was Anton Webern.

6. The composers Erik Satie and Charles Ives shared several traits.

7. The music of Béla Bartók was influenced by his musicological research into the music of Heinrich Isaac.

8. The communist philosophy in the Soviet Union in the 1930s and 1940s tended to foster a conservative musical style.

9. Jazz included elements of African-American and Western traditional musics.

10. The composers Luigi Russolo, George Antheil, Edgard Varèse, Henry Cowell, Harry Partch, and John Cage were known as the "six."

Short Essay

Identify at least three major European composers who emigrated to the United States in the period between World War I and World War II. Explain what music styles and ideas each one represented.

Discuss at least two examples in the music of the 1920s, 1930s, and 1940s in which composers adopted radically new styles that resulted in music that would challenge the public's assumptions and tastes, and two examples of music in the same period that reached out to the public's tastes and abilities.

ANSWERS TO SAMPLE TEST QUESTIONS

Multiple Choice

1. D   Arnold Schoenberg
2. E   retrograde inversion
3. E   Anton Webern
4. B   objectivity
5. B   France
6. A   Gebrauchsmusik
7. D   socialist realism
8. C   Aaron Copland
9. D   George Gershwin
10. D   avant-garde

True-False/Justification

1. F   The twelve-tone method was conceived as a way of producing control and order in atonal music.

2. F   Twelve pitch classes can be ordered in 12 factorial or 479,001,600 ways.

3. T   Twelve-tone and non–twelve-tone materials are brought together in such works as Schoenberg's Variations for Orchestra, op. 31, and Berg's Violin Concerto.

4. F   Klangfarbenmelodie refers to the pointillistic use of instrumentation; the seamless style of musical structure was called "unendliche Melodie" by Wagner.

5. T   Webern was unlikely to combine serial and nonserial materials; his rows themselves are constructed in the most carefully ordered fashion; and he extended the serial idea to other elements of music besides pitch.

6. T   Both Satie and Ives were experimental composers, and both employed iconoclastic wit in their works.

7. F   Bartók was an ethnomusicologist, and his style was influenced by his research in folk music. (Webern wrote a dissertation on Isaac.)

8. T   Socialist realism argued that the composer's work should be understandable by the masses and rejected modernism as formalist.

9. T   African-American elements in jazz included syncopated rhythms and improvisational technique, while the Western tradition contributed textural and harmonic patterns.

10. F   Russolo, Antheil, Varèse, Cowell, Partch, and Cage were all avant-garde composers; the "six" were French neoclassic composers.

CHAPTER 24

IN THE SECOND HALF OF THE TWENTIETH CENTURY

CHAPTER OVERVIEW

After World War II the further development of serialism produced total control music, in which the composer's precompositional planning determined the details of the musical sound.

Experiments in the area of timbre led to extended techniques on existing instruments and voice. The new problems presented by both these directions of musical development lent themselves to electronic solutions by means of first tape recorders and other studio equipment, then synthesizers and computers.

Reacting against the movement to total control, some composers have explored the possibilities of indeterminacy in music, leaving some aspects of their compositions open to chance or to decisions by the performer. New types of musical structure have been produced by minimalism and process music, in which limited amounts of tone material generate music through some sort of more or less systematic procedure.

In the second half of the twentieth century, composers have also created performance-oriented music and combined music with other forms of art. These experiments allow for the expression of the composers's philosophical viewpoints and help to increase the appeal of radically new styles to audiences.

Jazz and popular music have increased in sophistication toward the end of the century. Historical developments of style can already be traced within these genres, as well as a fragmentation of styles which parallels that within the "serious" Western musical tradition. The Western musical tradition has begun to open up in some senses. Women composers and composers from non-white races and non-Western cultural backgrounds have begun to find a place for their musical expressions in Western culture.

The diversification of ideas and styles in the Western musical tradition and the apparent abandonment of literary models for musical expression in the twentieth century suggest that this period may form the beginning of a major new era in music history.

OBJECTIVES

1. To introduce the student to the extension of earlier ideas into the styles of total control music and to the use of extended techniques in music.

2. To familiarize the student with the different possibilities of electronic music composition.

3. To give the student an understanding of the aesthetic bases of and approaches to the new musical procedures of indeterminacy, minimalism and process music, and performance music.

4. To encourage the student to consider the nature of Western musical culture in the late twentieth century.

TERMS, NAMES, AND CONCEPTS

total control
Milton Babbitt
Olivier Messiaen
nonretrogradable rhythms
Pierre Boulez
Institut de Recherche et de Coordination Acoustique/Musique
Darmstadt Summer Course for New Music
Karlheinz Stockhausen
extended techniques
Krzysztof Penderecki
George Crumb
electronic music
Columbia-Princeton Electronic Music Center
Otto Luening
Vladimir Ussachevsky
tape music
musique concrète
Pierre Schaeffer
Pierre Henry
synthesizer sine, square, sawtooth waves
"white" noise
filtering
reverberation
overdubbing
tape loop
computer music
Charles Dodge
Mario Davidovsky
indeterminacy, chance music, aleatory music
4'33"
Lejaren Hiller
Yannis Xenakis

minimalism
systematic music, process music
Terry Riley
Steve Reich
performance music
mixed media
Philip Glass
George Rochberg
New Romanticism
bop
Charlie Parker
Dizzy Gillespie
free jazz
John Coltranc
Ornette Coleman
third stream
Gunther Schuller
rhythm and blues
country-western music
rock and roll
The Beatles
Frank Zappa
Ellen Taaffe Zwilich
William Grant Still
T. J. Anderson
Ravi Shankar
Toru Takemitsu

CLASSROOM APPROACHES, ASSIGNMENTS, TOPICS FOR DISCUSSION

Total Control, Extended Techniques, and Indeterminacy

Students may be interested in composing short pieces of their own, using the principles of either total serialization or indeterminacy. It may help them to do so if they narrow the range of possibilities by using limited tone materials other than those of traditional instruments. They should perform and explain their pieces in class. Discuss what problems and advantages these styles present to the composer, to the performer, and to the listener.

Electronic Music

Students should be at least somewhat familiar with electronic resources for composition. Arrange a demonstration in an electronic studio or with a synthesizer in the classroom to introduce the fundamental types of timbre and compositional techniques available with electronic means.

Discuss with students some aesthetic and social questions raised by electronic composition and media. Is the elimination of the live performer a significant loss to the musical experience? What effect does the replacement of performances in public gatherings by private hearing of recorded music have on musical and social life?

Minimalism and Process Music

Arrange a performance in class of Steve Reich's "Clapping Music" (for scores, see ATCM, 161–162 and MTC, 251–253). Discuss the nature of the musical material and the process that produces the phasing of the two parts. What are the principal things that the listener perceives as the music unfolds?

Assign students to compose a piece of process music for performance in class. Have the members of the class describe what they have heard. Ask them to list what traditional musical concepts and analytical terminology can and cannot be applied to this music.

Popular Music

Ask students to bring to class a variety of recordings of different types of popular music. Play the recordings, and ask students to identify connections of these pieces with earlier music in the Western tradition in terms of (1) topics, (2) style characteristics, (3) place within the historical development of the style (i.e., early, late; conservative, progressive; Apollonian-objective-classic, Dionysian-subjective-romantic.

Discuss with students the cultural position of popular music in the second half of the twentieth century. In what ways does the situation of modern popular music differ from that of popular music in earlier centuries? Can modern popular music be clearly separated from art music, and are the divisions among popular styles less significant than those that separate popular from "serious" music? How do the varied styles within popular music and between popular and "serious" music contribute to social divisions in modern Western culture?

MUSIC FOR STUDY

Olivier Messiaen (b. 1908), Quatuor pour la fin du temps, *VI. Danse de la fureur, pour les sept trompettes*

Style features

The quartet includes violin, clarinet, cello, and piano. This movement, because it is simply scored in octaves for all four instruments together clearly reveals Messiaen's complex rhythmic techniques.

Score

ATCM, 152–160

Krzysztof Penderecki (b. 1933), Threnody for the Victims of Hiroshima

Style features

The main interest in the *Threnody* arises from timbre and dynamics rather than rhythm and pitch. The work uses extended performance techniques for the orchestra of 52 string instruments. Unusual timbral effects are also produced by the closely clustered frequencies.

Score

AAM, 845–851—excerpt

George Crumb (b. 1929), Ancient Voices of Children, V. *Se ha llenado de luces mi corazón de seda*

Style features

The scoring is for soprano, boy soprano, percussion, mandolin, oboe, and piano. Special devices, amplification, and extended techniques are called for. The texture changes frequently.

The piece seems somewhat improvisatory, since some rhythms are performed very freely and some pitches are largely indeterminate.

The treatment of the text is highly expressive and atmospheric.

This work includes some visual and gestural components. Performers move on and off the stage, and the composer suggests the addition of dance or mime.

Score

AMSS, 521–527

Pauline Oliveros (b. 1932), Sonic Meditations, *excerpts*

Style features

The music consists of activities prescribed in prose instructions to the performers. The instructions include the participants' physical placement, sound production, and listening.

Score

HAMW, 364–366—includes *Meditations* I, XIV, XV

Terry Riley (b. 1935), In C

Style features

The minimalist piece consists of 53 short pitch and rhythmic motives, together with a steady pulse of repeated notes c ^{4} and c ^{5} played on the piano. The exact scoring, dynamics, the rate of each performer's progress from each motive to the next, and the length of any performance remain indeterminate. Harmony and texture arise empirically within each playing of the work.

Scores

AAM, 872–874

SSHS 2, 452–453

Ellen Taaffe Zwilich (b. 1939), Symphony No. 1 (Three Movements for Orchestra), first movement

Style features

Zwilich employs a large and colorful orchestra. The movement develops organically from the cell or motto consisting of a minor third, introduced at the beginning. The music is clearly shaped as a large arch by its dynamic. The harmony is freely dissonant, though the pitch center A serves as a clear point of tonal orientation.

Score

HAMW, 375–401

SAMPLE TEST QUESTIONS

Multiple Choice

1. Total control in music developed from the principles of _____ as an approach to composition.

    A. the avant-garde
    B. drama
    C. jazz
    D. neoclassicism
    E. serialism

2. A nonretrogradable rhythm is one in which the durations are arranged to form a(n) _____.

    A. series
    B. palindrome

    C. ostinato
    D. sine wave
    E. agrément

3. Uses of unconventional methods of producing sound from the voice or orchestral instruments are generally referred to as _____.

    A. aleatory music
    B. extended techniques
    C. musique concrète
    D. process music
    E. shakuhachi

4. Music composed by the manipulation of tape-recorded "live" sounds is known as _____.

    A. Klangfarbenmelodie
    B. musique concrète
    C. overdubbing
    D. third stream music
    E. chance music

5. A(n) _____ helps a composer produce serial music in an electronic studio.

    A. Darmstadt
    B. Stockhausen
    C. tape loop
    D. biwa
    E. alea

6. John Cage was one of the leading figures in the employment of _____ in music.

    A. synthesizers
    B. total control
    C. jazz
    D. mathematics
    E. indeterminacy

7. The music of the movement known as _____ employs a number of techniques deliberately intended to create public appeal in new music.

    A. New Romanticism
    B. serialism
    C. computer music
    D. bop
    E. fragmentation

8. In the 1950s the style of rhythm and blues combined with country-western music to produce _____.

   A. total control
   B. rock and roll
   C. third stream music
   D. free jazz
   E. New Romanticism

9. Rock music, the tradition of Stravinsky, and the avant-garde are combined in the music of _____.

   A. Dizzy Gillespie
   B. John Cage
   C. the Beatles
   D. Toru Takemitsu
   E. Frank Zappa

10. John Coltrane and Ornette Coleman contributed to the development of the musical style of _____.

    A. New Romanticism
    B. rock and roll
    C. total control
    D. computer music
    E. free jazz

True-False/Justification

1. Milton Babbitt's musical technique stems from his background as a poet.

2. The city of Darmstadt in Germany became an important center for new music after World War II.

3. Extended techniques are applied exclusively to acoustical instruments and do not involve electronics.

4. The composition of aleatory music requires the use of dice.

5. Phasing is an important musical feature in third stream music .

6. The concept of the Gesamtkunstwerk has been applied to advanced musical genres in the late twentieth century.

7. Since the Beatles came to the United States from England, their music represents the earliest phase of rhythm and blues.

8. The Western musical tradition has been infiltrated by foreign influence in the end of the twentieth century.

9. The first electronic music was composed before 1950.

10. Western musical culture in the late twentieth century is not characterized by unity in its musical style.

Short Essay

Discuss ways in which musical styles in the years since World War II have challenged earlier assumptions about the position of (1) the performer and (2) the listener.

Explain three examples of the influence of non-Western music on the music in the Western tradition since 1950.

ANSWERS TO SAMPLE TEST QUESTIONS

Multiple Choice

1. E   serialism
2. B   palindrome
3. B   extended techniques
4. B   musique concrete
5. C   tape loop
6. E   indeterminacy
7. A   New Romanticism
8. B   rock and roll
9. E   Frank Zappa
10. E   free jazz

True-False/Justification

1. F   Babbitt began as a mathematician and applied mathematical procedures in his music.

2. T   Darmstadt was the location of a summer course set up to introduce German composers to the latest musical techniques.

3. F   Among the possibilities for the application of extended techniques is the addition of electronic devices to standard instruments.

4. F   Although the derivation of the term aleatory comes from the Latin word for dice, aleatory music can be produced by a wide variety of random procedures.

5. F   Phasing is a process associated with minimalism.

6. T   Combined art works since 1950 include mixed-media works and the rock music video.

7. F   The Beatles belong to a fully developed stage in the history of rock music.

8. T   African drumming and Indian drumming and sitar music have affected both popular and serious composers, and composers such as Messiaen and Takemitsu combine Western and non-Western musical materials.

9. T   The earliest tape music dates from 1948.

10. T   There has been considerable fragmentation of musical culture since 1950 in serious and popular styles.

Name:_____

SCORE/LISTENING WORKSHEET

Composer (dates):_____

Piece (date):_____

Style period:_____ Genre:_____

Scoring

    Performers:_____

    _____

    Special effects:_____

    _____

    Comments:_____

    _____

Dynamics and other expressive markings:_____

_____

Rhythm

    Meter:_____ Tempo:_____

    Special devices (label in score):_____

    _____

Melody

    Principal theme (label in score):_____

    _____
    _____
    _____
    _____

    Location:_____ Range:_____ to_____

    Motion:_____ Shape:_____

Secondary theme (label in score):_____

_____
_____
_____
_____

    Location:_____   Range:_____ to _____

    Motion:_____   Shape:_____

    Other theme (label in score):_____

_____
_____
_____
_____

    Location:_____   Range:_____ to _____

    Motion:_____   Shape:_____

Harmony (label individual harmonies in score)

    Tonality:_____

    Patterns:_____

    Comments:_____

    _____

Texture:_____

Form:_____

Diagram (label divisions in score):

Text treatment:_____

_____

_____

List of Transparencies

1. The Greater Perfect System
2. Medieval Cantus Firmus Texture
3. Isorhythm: Tenor of Guillaume de Machaut, "Maugre mon cuer/De ma dolour/Quia amore langueo"
4. Renaissance Textures: Fuga (Imitation), Paired Duets, Familiar Style
5. Baroque Monodic Texture with Basso Continuo; Baroque Trio Texture
6. Concerto Grosso Scoring
7. Relationships Among Renaissance and Baroque Genres
8. A. Binary Form (overlay for B and C)
   B. Rounded [Binary Form]
   C. [Binary] Sonata [Form]
9. Relationship Among Baroque, Classic, and Romantic Genres
10. The Periods of the Western Musical Tradition

1 The Greater Perfect System

Seaton, *Ideas and Styles in the Western Musical Tradition.*
©1991 Mayfield Publishing Company

2 Medieval Cantus Firmus Texture

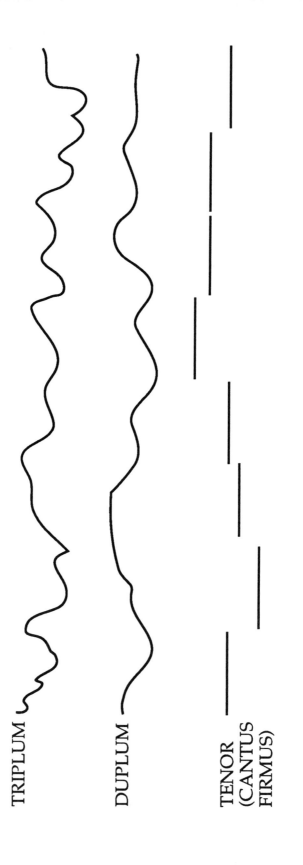

TRIPLUM

DUPLUM

TENOR
(CANTUS
FIRMUS)

Seaton, Ideas and Styles in the Western Musical Tradition. ©1991 Mayfield Publishing Company

3 Isorhythm
Tenor of Guillaume de Machaut, "Maugre mon cuer/De ma dolour/Quia amore langueo"

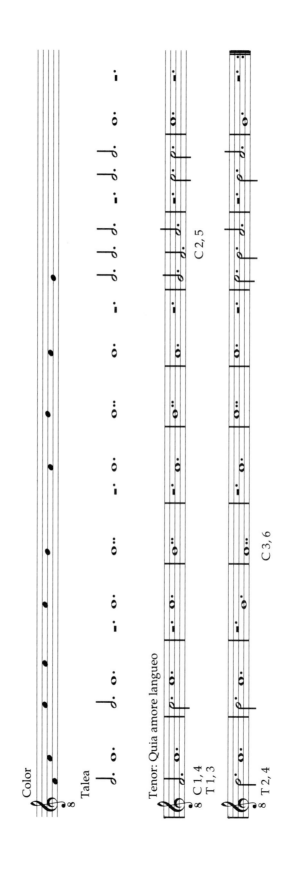

Seaton, *Ideas and Styles in the Western Musical Tradition.* ©1991 Mayfield Publishing Company

4 Renaissance Textures
Fuga (Imitation), Paired Duets, Familiar Style

Seaton, *Ideas and Styles in the Western Musical Tradition*. ©1991 Mayfield Publishing Company

5 Baroque Monodic Texture with Basso Continuo

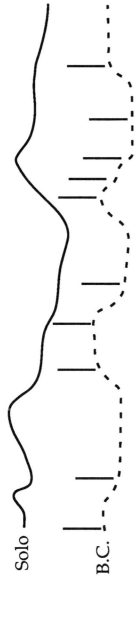

Solo

B.C.

Baroque Trio Texture

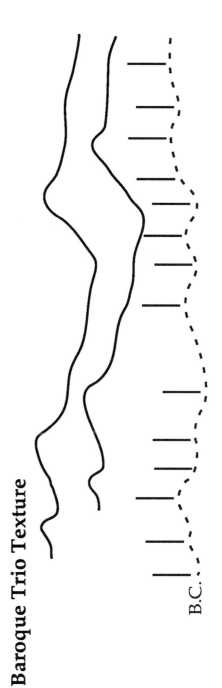

B.C.

Seaton, Ideas and Styles in the Western Musical Tradition. ©1991 Mayfield Publishing Company

6 Concerto Grosso Scoring

Tutti Concertino Tutti Concertino Tutti

Seaton, *Ideas and Styles in the Western Musical Tradition.* ©1991 Mayfield Publishing Company

7   Relationships Among Renaissance and Baroque Genres

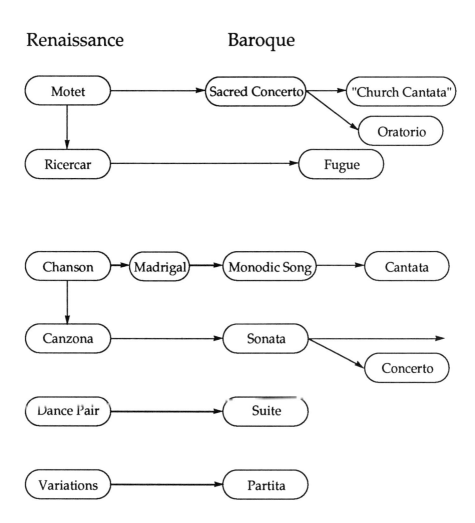

Renaissance   Baroque

Motet → Sacred Concerto → "Church Cantata"

Sacred Concerto → Oratorio

Motet → Ricercar

Ricercar → Fugue

Chanson → Madrigal → Monodic Song → Cantata

Chanson → Canzona

Canzona → Sonata

Sonata → Concerto

Dance Pair → Suite

Variations → Partita

Seaton, *Ideas and Styles in the Western Musical Tradition.*
©1991 Mayfield Publishing Company

8a

**Binary
Form**

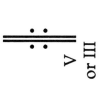

I
or i

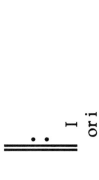

V
or III

I
or i

Seaton, *Ideas and Styles in the Western Musical Tradition.* ©1991 Mayfield Publishing Company

8b Rounded

P

P
⌒
I
or i

Seaton, Ideas and Styles in the Western Musical Tradition. ©1991 Mayfield Publishing Company

8c

Sonata

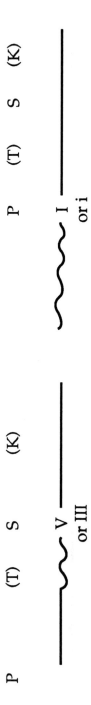

P	(T)	S	(K)		P	(T)	S	(K)

V or III   I or i

Seaton, *Ideas and Styles in the Western Musical Tradition*. ©1991 Mayfield Publishing Company

9 Relationships Among Baroque, Classic, and Romantic Genres

Baroque   Classic   Romantic

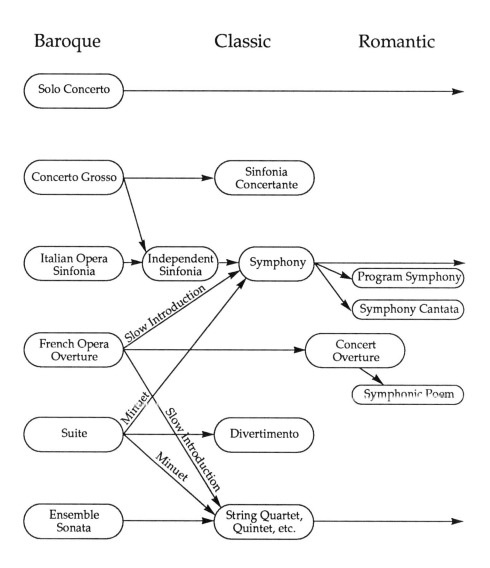

Seaton, *Ideas and Styles in the Western Musical Tradition.*
©1991 Mayfield Publishing Company

10 The Periods of the Western Musical Tradition

Mathematical Model	Literary Models for Musical Expression			?
	Poetry	Rhetoric	Drama	
Middle Ages	Renaissance	Baroque	Classic — Romantic	Twentieth Century
Age of Faith	Humanism	Rationalism	Enlightenment : Revolution	Age of Technology

Seaton, *Ideas and Styles in the Western Musical Tradition*. ©1991 Mayfield Publishing Company